## Authors' Biographies

### Pastor David Witt, the

Spirit of Martyrdom ministries, has over 2,000 churches and Christian ministries in the United States, traveled throughout Canada and Mexico, visited thirteen countries in Europe, and spent three weeks in Israel at the Holy Land Institute for Biblical Studies.

He has been associated as a representative with the ministry of The Voice of the Martyrs for over a decade. His heart has been touched, and his life changed, by their actions of love and faithfulness to Jesus, even when facing death.

He reports, "During the last 30 years more Muslims have found faith in the Lord Jesus Christ than the combined number of converts of the last fourteen hundred years of Islam." As David has traveled he has met hundreds of Muslims with stories of finding faith in Christ. In this book he not only exposes the religious justification for the Islamic martyrdom of hatred and violence, but also shares over 50 overcoming stories of Christians living with fearless love.

### Dr. Mujahid El Masih has studied Islam and the Qur'an for over

14 years in Pakistan. In 1997 persecution peaked against his faith and he had to flee Pakistan. Pastor Masih shares, "I did not find Jesus but Jesus Christ found me and used me to start churches in Pakistan." Now there are nearly one hundred churches, a Bible school, a medical clinic, and a child-support program in Pakistan. His ministry has presently expanded to Asia and Africa.

He has traveled to 42 states here in the USA, and has spoken in over 600 churches of all sizes. Pastor Masih has also spoken at Focus on the Family in Colorado Springs, Pastor John Piper's church in Minneapolis, Minnesota, the national conference for The Voice of the Martyrs, and many regional conferences. He has spoken on Christian television programs, Moody Radio, American Family, and other radio programs. He has given many conferences and seminars on Islam including Colorado Christian University, Biola, Masters College, North Central University, University of Montana, Missoula and many others.

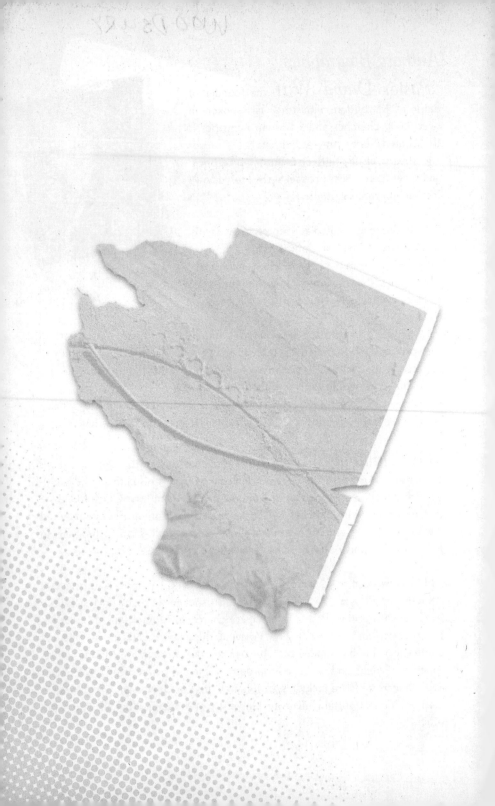

# FEARLESS LOVE
## Rediscovering Jesus' Spirit of Martyrdom

With Meditations of Christ and His Love

David Witt
Mujahid El Masih

**Published By Martus Publishing**
**PO Box 101 Clarkdale, AZ 86324**

We desire to learn and hear your comments or testimony regarding this book. You can e-mail us at comments@SpiritOfMartyrdom.com

spirit of
martyrdom
acts 1:8 — you will be my witnesses

Distributed by:
Martus Publishing
PO Box 101
Clarkdale, AZ 86324
contact@SpiritofMartyrdom.com


Layout and Format completed by
Jay Myers at The Yetsirah Company
www.yetsirah.com

ISBN 978-0-615-24033-6
Printed in the United States of America

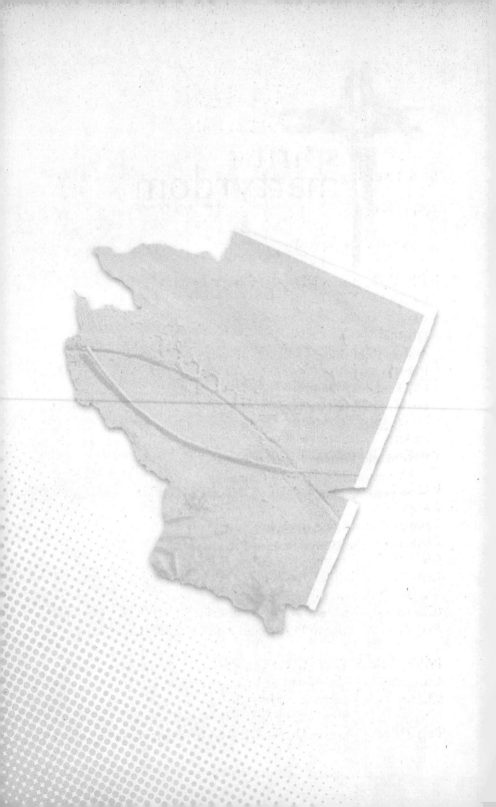

# TABLE
## *Of Contents*

BIOGRAPHIES                                           01

FOREWORD                                              11

ACKNOWLEDGEMENTS                                      13

PART ONE: ISLAMIC MARTYRDOM,                          17
THE CALL OF ALLAH (JIHAD)
Note to Christian and Muslim Friends                 19
Chapter 1a    Why, And How To Use This Book          23
Chapter 1     Faithful Unto Death                    29
Chapter 2     Jihad-The Great Commission             33
Chapter 3     Muslims To Fight Until
              All Their Opponents Submit             39
Chapter 4     Silent Jihad                           49
Chapter 5     Jihad For Personal Salvation           55
Part One      **Group Discussion And Contemplation**     58

PART TWO: A JIHADIST CHANGED BY JESUS                63
Chapter 6     Pakistan - Homes On Fire               65
Chapter 7     Growing Up In Pakistan                 69
Chapter 8     Becoming a Muslim                      73
Chapter 9     Running From God                       77
Chapter 10    Called To Pastor                       81
Chapter 11    Attack by Muslim Mobs                  85
Chapter 12    Persecution in South Africa            89
Part Two      **Group Discussion And Contemplation**     94

PART THREE: LIVING MARTYRS                           99
Chapter 13    The Advancing Persecuted Church        101
Chapter 14    Suffering For His Glory                109
Chapter 15    What Is Lacking In Christ's Afflictions    115
Part Three    **Group Discussion And Contemplation**     120

# Table Of Contents...

**PART FOUR: DYING TO SHARE JESUS**                                 125
Chapter 16     Blood Of The Martyrs In Pakistan                     127
Chapter 17     Martyrs Of Sudan                                     133
Chapter 18     The Cross: Symbol Of What?                           137
Chapter 19     Martyrdom In America                                 143
**Part Four     Group Discussion And Contemplation**                150


**PART FIVE:**
**INDUSTRUCTABLE-NOT A SECOND TO LOSE**                             155
Chapter 20     Bombing Of Baghdad                                   157
Chapter 21     God Has Ordained Our Days                            161
Chapter 22     God Is Fully Sovereign                               164
**Part Five     Group Discussion And Contemplation**                169


**PART SIX: REWARDS OF THE MARTYRS**                                173
Chapter 23     The Great Debate                                     175
Chapter 24     Biblical Rewards in Heaven                           179
Chapter 25     Condition of the Christian Martyrs In Heaven         185
**Part Six      Group Discussion And Contemplation**                190


**PART SEVEN: FOR THE LOVE OF MUSLIMS**                             195
Chapter 26     Egyptian Muslim Finds Peace:
               Witnessing Steps 1-3                                 197
Chapter 27     Guidance Of The Holy Spirit:
               Witnessing Steps 4-7                                 203
Chapter 28     Miracles: Witnessing Steps 8-11                      209
Chapter 29     Use Godly Wisdom: Witnessing Steps 12-17             215
**Part Seven    Group Discussion And Contemplation**                219


**APPENDIX: SPIRITUAL FOUNDATIONS OF ISLAM**                        225
**Appendix       Group Discussion And Contemplation**               237


**FINAL NOTE: COME LET US REASON TOGETHER**                         241
About the Cover Photo                                               245

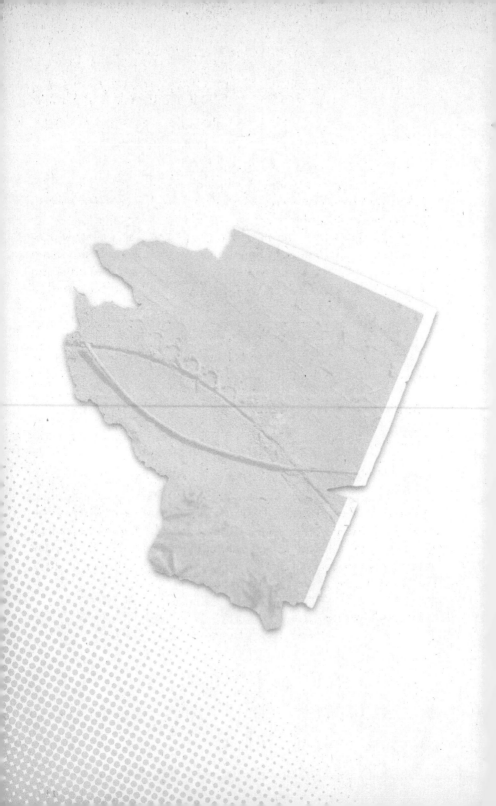

# FOREWORD
### by Tom White:

We appreciate David and Mujahid's energy, zeal and heart for the persecuted church. You will find that reflected in this work, which contrasts Biblical martyrdom with Islamic martyrdom.

Utilizing verses from the Bible and the Qur'an, this series includes powerful personal testimonies from former Muslims who are now living their lives for Christ. Done with respect, honesty and authority, the series is informative for Christians, as well as a very honorable appeal to Muslims to seek Jesus. The Spirit of Martyrdom could be used to share with a Muslim, as an apologetics tool for Christians or to gain prayer material when praying for Muslims.

I wish David and Mujahid well in their desire to awaken and alert the Body of Christ with this work.

**Tom White**
**Executive Director**
**The Voice of the Martyrs**

"I learned so much from this book! People often ask me, 'What can we do about "this Muslim problem?"' David and Mujahid have explained the Biblical theology of 'loving your enemies' very well. Loving our enemies may be messy and costly, but it is what we are called to do. May God grant that we become martyrs of love!"

**Gracia Burnham**
**Author of** In The Presence Of My Enemies, and To Fly Again.

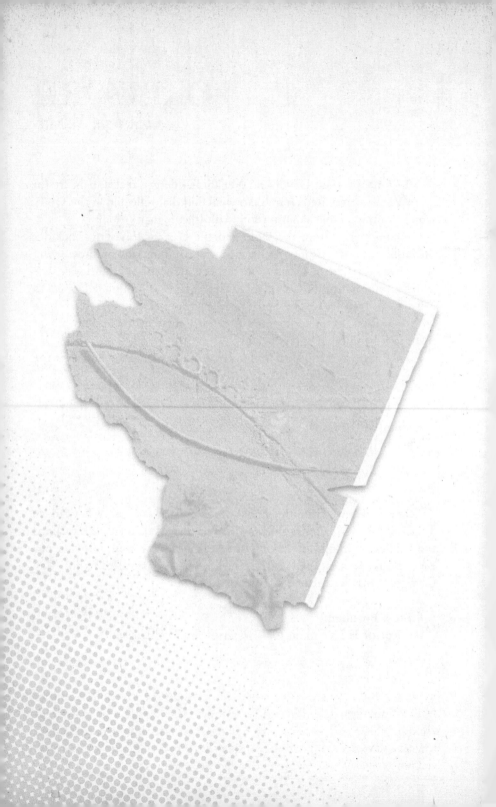

*Acknowledgements*
# A TRIBUTE
*To Fearless Lovers*

Mujahid and I (David) want to acknowledge the team of people who made this book possible. First, I want to thank my bride Cindy for the great sacrifice of time and editing along with my children Jonathan and Kaitlyn for their encouragement and prayers. The "beyond the call" wisdom and financial investment from my parents Bill and Shari. This book would not have been possible without the work and coaching of our editor Joy Gage and her husband Ken. The graphic and format contribution of Jay Myers is a true inspiration from God. I want to thank Jay's wife Raynna for her sacrifice and support of her husband and the ministry of Spirit of Martyrdom.

I want to thank the Board of Directors of Spirit of Martyrdom and specifically Jim Ledbetter, John Mahon, and Angela Windsor for the many hours and generous leadership they have offered. We owe a great debt of love to the leadership of The Voice of the Martyrs and the staff. We could name everyone on staff for all have been a blessing. Especially we want to express our gratitude for the support offered by Executive Director Tom White, my friendship and leadership coach Paul Gustafson. Thank you for the leadership, and friendship from Jim and Peggy Dau, Dave and Cheryl Brackemyre. We want to especially recognize the dedication, faithful friend and management of Matt Rose who was our supervisor for ten years with The Voice of the Martyrs. Special tribute is due to Burton Swartz who is now living in the presence of our Lord Jesus and his lovely wife Evangeline who were the first ones to encourage me to complete this book. Tim and Darcie Gill, Robert Brock, Tom Tremble, Getaneh have been our co-laborers, speaking and traveling with testimonies of the persecuted Church. The appreciation we have for their lives and ministries is beyond words.

Very well, the true foundations for this book are the prayer warriors. First, we want to thank JoAnna Chandler. She has labored for us in prayer for over a decade. Her reward in heaven is great. She has become part of our family. Thank you to the prayer team of nearly one hundred whom I e-mail every week. Thank you for the amazing love, support and prayers I have received from my in-laws Bob and Marie O'Connell and Mel and Gwen Wait. My extended family members' encouragement at

## Acknowledgements

many moments in the journey include
Leif, Heather and Ashley Edon; Rob,
Debbie, Christina, Austin and Andrew Witt;
Wesley and Liddie Witt. I owe love and gratitude
to my Bible study guys who have continued to support and
encourage me. Especially I want to thank Bill Hickey for his
contribution in the completion of this book with his insightful
feedback and suggestions. My pastor, Robb Williams, who only took
the leadership of my home church two years ago and from the first day
has stood behind me. Thanks for my Sunday school teacher Jim Ayers.
The years of faithful support to help me at this point of life come from
Larry and Linda Peterson, Tom and Sandy Sharp, Ron and Lois Pollard,
and Montie and Heidi Fortkamp. We also thank Len and Jan Turner,
Mark and Maggie Hillis, Mike and Jody McRoberts. I want to thank one
of my newest friends and supporters Ray and Bobbie Roles who in the
final stages of this book helped complete the project. There are many
others I could name and God knows of their contribution.

Of course this list of heroes would not be complete without mentioning
my special friendship with Mujahid El Masih who is like a blood brother
to me. This book certainly would not have been possible without his
collaboration. My life is ultimately dedicated with gratitude to my
Heaven Father, my Lord and Savior Jesus Christ and my comforter and
guide the Holy Spirit.

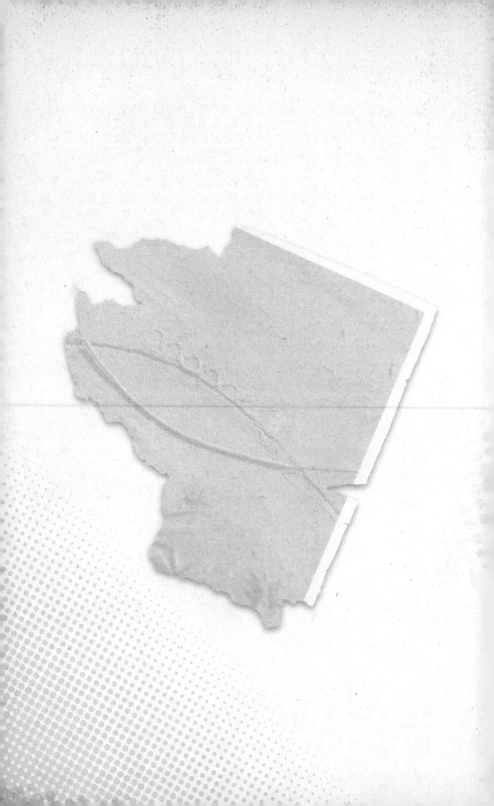

# Part One:
# ISLAMIC MARTYRDOM
## The Call of Allah (Jihad)

*Fearless Love Notes:*

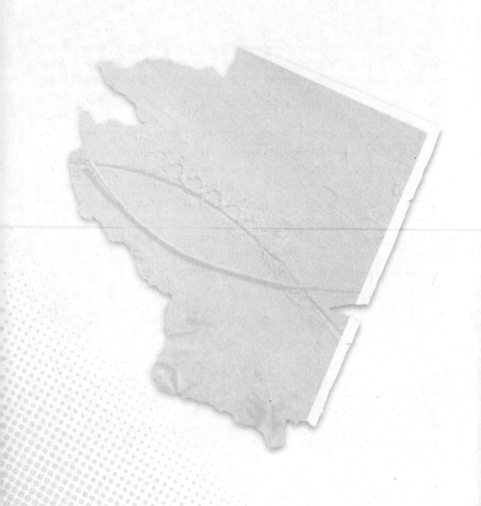

# NOTE TO CHRISTIAN
## *and Muslim Friends*

Salaam (Peace) dear friend,

We are delighted that you are reading this book. We hope it will raise some important questions in your mind, as well as provide some significant answers. Does the violence in our world and within Islam among fundamentalist Muslims disturb you? Are you perplexed that the adherents of a religion claiming to be peaceful can act so destructively and claim to do so in the name of Allah? Are you angered about the terrorism and suicide bombers by the so called martyrs? Are you aware that "martyr" is an important ideal in both Islam and Christianity, but that the meaning of the word in each religion is diametrically opposed. Have you seen hypocrisy among Muslims and Christians alike? You are not alone! Jesus, condemned the religious leaders of his day for similar issues calling them a "brood of vipers," "whitewashed tombs" and "hypocrites." In the Bible, John 13:35 states: "By this all men will know that you are My disciples, if you have love for one another."

As we meet people from different parts of the world, we see a hunger and a thirst for peace and a yearning to experience authentic love. Jesus, the Prince of Peace, explains "I Am the Way, the Truth, and the Life, no one comes to the Father except through Me." (John 14:6)

In this book we invite you to consider a few issues: Is Islamic martyrdom the greatest hope of peace for you and people everywhere? Christ told his disciples to love their enemies and to return good to those who do evil.

Wouldn't the greatest act of martyrdom be to love your enemies and die in the pursuit of bringing them love? Someone has said, "We can avoid making up our minds, but we cannot avoid making up our lives." In this perspective, we must all choose what is greater; dying as a martyr for Allah and fighting the enemies of Islam, or dying and living as a martyr for Christ by freely laying down our lives for the benefit of our enemies.

If by the end of this book you are convinced that love is the greatest power, then we invite you to surrender your life to the Lord Jesus Christ. True peace and love will enter your heart. You will join thousands of other Christians around the world and Muslims who have been transformed by a loving relationship with the Lord Jesus Christ. In the pages to follow you will hear some of their stories.

You will also understand why this book is written mainly for Christians. We are calling all Christians to consider a Biblical martyrdom by laying down their lives for the love of Muslims.

May peace be upon you,

Dawoud (Arabic for David) and Mujahid (Warrior)

John 13:35

"By this all men will know that you are my disciples, if you love one another."

۳۵ بِهٰذَا يَعْرِفُ الْجَمِيعُ أَنَّكُمْ تَلَامِيذِي: إِنْ كَانَ لَكُمْ حُبٌّ بَعْضًا لِبَعْضٍ».

*Fearless Love Notes:*

# WHY AND HOW
## *To Use This Book*

Fear is the greatest block to the freedom of love and life. Christ came to bring freedom from the fear of suffering and death. What is the antidote to fear? It is love! "Love casts out fear." (1 John 4:18) The scripture goes on to tell us, "the one who fears is not perfected in love." In other words, when God's children mature in love they have less fear. When fear grows it drives out love. "Fearless love" means less fear and more love. It is the essence of courage.

> *"Fearless love" means less fear and more love. It is the essence of courage.*

This book has teaching and stories regarding Biblical martyrdom, Islamic martyrdom and persecution. But do not be intimidated. These are powerful subjects and they are written with the intent to bless you and change your life forever. It is first written for Christians who are looking for purpose and hope in these days of world-wide terrorism and second for Muslims seeking the heart of God in true worship. Our hope is that the fruit of this book will produce a fearless love to help you enjoy the journey of an obedient life that God intends for all His children.

What is "The Spirit of Martyrdom?" Acts 1:8 records the words of Jesus, "but you will receive power when the Holy Spirit has come upon you; and you shall be My witnesses both in Jerusalem, and in all Judea and Samaria, and even to the remotest part of the earth." Christ says MY WITNESSES. The word here for witnesses in the Greek is "martus." It is where we get our modern English word "martyr." Jesus is literally saying you shall be "My Martyrs." Christ wants His martyrs to be lovers who sacrifice and risk for others. The spirit of martyrdom is Christ's Holy Spirit of love indwelling in His children. It is a love so great that fear dissipates and joy abounds in doing the right thing, even when the cost is great.

This is a "Rediscovery" of the spirit of martyrdom because Christ's Holy Spirit has always been with His Church. The spirit of martyrdom is the heart of God and a theme of scripture. In modern history many have forgotten or lost the depth of this characteristic of God, so much that many people today have a difficult time even remembering how to spell "martyr."

Do we have your attention yet? Read on. We promise not to disappoint as we contrast Islamic martyrdom with Biblical martyrdom. While the subject of death, persecution and Islamic martyrdom can be difficult and even scary; we encourage you to persevere. Ultimately you will find in the following pages hope, faith and a depth of love that most people have never considered let alone lived out.

### Individual, Church, and Small Group Study Help

*For Individuals:*

We designed this book to be user friendly and provided many options that can be used in different contexts. It was developed to be used by individuals and/or groups. We broke the chapters into bite sizes to help absorb the material. The book has eight parts which breaks down to 30 chapters when including the Appendix. Therefore, a reader can choose to read this book in little over a week, covering a part every day or for a more thoughtful pace we have created short chapters, which can be enjoyed by reading one chapter a day for a month. Most readers can read our chapters in five to fifteen minutes. We have included a meditation at the end of every chapter. Every meditation is focused on God's love in light of the subject material.

Eight discussion guides are included at the end of every part.

*For Churches:*

We invite Churches to use this book in their small groups as an eight week study. This study will first expose the doctrine of Islamic jihad to the average Christian. Christians need to understand the depth of the problem and the conflict ahead for the Church. The conflict between fundamental Islam and the West is not going away. We hope every Church in America might use this book as a text to enlighten their congregation and help lead Christians to a loving Biblical response.

*For Small Groups:*

For a small group study we recommend that every participant purchase a book. Each week a group should study one Part. The divisions of the book are seven Parts plus an Appendix which should take most groups eight weeks to complete. Encourage everyone to read a chapter a day and then meditate on the reading during the week. We suggest that every small group purchase the audio book. Short sections can be played at the meetings to help remind participants of the material, stimulate thoughts, and jump start the discussion time. We have suggested the sections of the audio book for you to play. We have laid out the discussion questions in a step by step format so that the least experienced facilitator can have easy success in guiding small group meetings. Little preparation is necessary for a very positive experience. What is most important is to let people come together and answer the questions put forth. The process of sharing will instill greater insight, memory and revelation. We suggest that a small group be no bigger than ten persons to help facilitate participation. The questions and small groups should only last one hour when following the guide and depending on the size of the group. If less time is needed use the even numbered questions only.

There is a wonderful synergy that comes out of group interaction. We hope that fresh ideas and action plans grow out of these communal studies. In fact, we want to hear how God uses these studies so please e-mail us with your testimonies at comments@SpiritofMartyrdom.com.

**One final notice** when the personal first person tense is used in the text by default it is David Witt speaking. When Mujahid speaks in first person the text will indicate the change.

### Fearless Love

This study will also help believers overcome their fear of Muslims as they discover what God is doing and God's love for the Muslim world. It will help Christians overcome their fear of suffering and death as they trust God in complete obedience and walk by faith in a spirit of fearless love. Another benefit is gaining a layman's understanding of the religious teachings of Islam as laid out in the Appendix. Last of all, we give 17 suggestions in Part Seven of how Christians can reach out with the love of Jesus to Muslims worldwide without ever leaving their home town. We pray that small groups might brainstorm projects of outreach that they can do as a team. The principles are universal in sharing God's love with people of all faiths and therefore we believe this book will help congregations grow in boldness and courage for their witness of Jesus Christ.

This is our testimony. Most of the stories are from our personal travels. The scriptures are from the insight God has given us in our journey of life. We have traveled many miles and met thousands of people. Our faith and understanding of the Kingdom of God has grown as we have

## Part One: Chapter 1a

heard and seen the stories of many lives. Most of the pictures used in this book have been taken by us. They are used with the permission of The Voice of the Martyrs (www.persecution.com) and The Spirit of Martyrdom ministries.

*Fearless Love Notes:*

*Fearless Love Notes:*

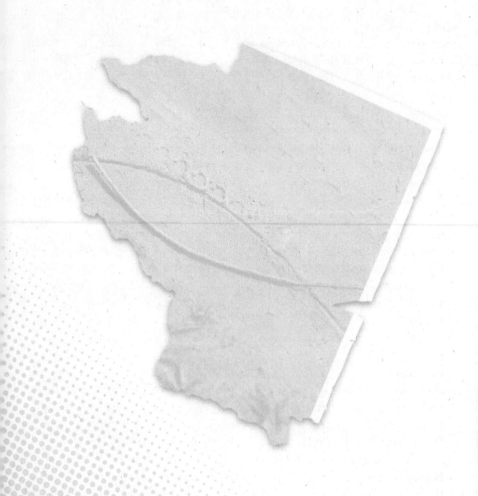

# FAITHFUL
## Unto Death

At 11p.m. on October 22, 2001, Sara a sixty-year-old Indonesian Christian woke up with a roaring sound above her. With alarm, Sara yelled to her husband Tio, "Pap, wake up! Where does the wind come from?" Tio responded, "Fire mama, the roof is on fire!" They immediately realized they were under attack from Muslims who are members of Laskar Jihad.

*Tio's village had been previously attacked. Many of the homes had been destroyed and only three families from their Church remained in the village.*

Laskar Jihad is the name of a fundamental Muslim organization for the training and implementing of jihad. In the last eight years Laskar Jihad and other Al Qaeda networks have been responsible for the destruction of over 1000 Churches, for burning thousands of homes and for the death of over 5,000 Christians. This is a "Holy War" for fundamental Muslims.

Indonesia has the largest Muslim population in the world. The "call to jihad" is powerful throughout Indonesia, but the "call of love" is even stronger!

Just a month before Tio's home burned, his granddaughter was playing in the jungle when she accidentally ran into several Muslim men training for "jihad". One of the men vehemently said, "Do not tell anyone about us or we will kill you!" These Muslim men were in training at a jihad encampment nearby. Little did Tio and Sara know, but this jihad compound had trained one of the men involved in the attack on the World Trade Center in New York City, September 11, 2001.

Tio's village had been previously attacked. Many of the homes had been destroyed and only three families from their Church remained in the village. During the first attack Tio and Sara stayed in their home and prayed. Thankfully, their home and the Church were spared. Tio was a man of principle and loved the Lord Jesus. He told Sara, "as long as the Church building remains, I will not leave the village." Tio was a deacon, he was the sole person left in the Church leadership. His determination remained steadfast.

# Part One: Chapter 1

Tio was approached several times to leave his Christian faith and to become a Muslim. The local primary school headmaster urged Tio to convert to Islam. When he refused, the Muslim man said, "I want to see whether you are of pure gold or fake gold." One week later, four Muslims came to Tio's home. One Muslim man said, "Pull those pictures of Jesus down!" Tio held true to his allegiance to the Lord and replied, "I will not take down those pictures, even if you behead me!" They were furious at Tio and told him that he would pay a price for his stubborn refusal.

In the middle of the night, Tio and Sara woke up to the sound of a roaring fire and the smell of the grass roof in flames. They ran out of their home with their granddaughter. Outside, people were running in a panic and many headed for the safety of the jungle nearby. Sara heard the attackers yelling "Allah Akbar," meaning Allah is Greater in Arabic. Tio could see that the Church was on fire too. He ran toward the burning Church, Sara and their granddaughter followed behind, with the hope to save it. Seeing the silhouette of the steeple in the starlight, Tio planned in his heart to rebuke the Muslims. Tio stood in front of the Church building ready to defend it. Suddenly, a Muslim man appeared with an automatic rifle. Shining his flashlight on Tio, he yelled, "Are you ready to die old man?" Tio answered fearlessly, "Yes, I am ready to die, but first let me pray!" The man cursed Tio, but allowed him to pray. With his arms stretched out toward Heaven, Tio prayed, "Dear Lord, do not punish this man, he does not know what he is doing. Please forgive him, Amen." Immediately, three shots rang out from the gunman striking Tio in the chest. Sara watched in horror, seizing the opportunity to escape, she grabbed her granddaughter and ran into the jungle.

In April, 2003 I had the privilege of meeting Sara. She lost everything in the attack. She shared with me about her husband's shocking death, and the difficult time hiding in the jungle. She continues to mourn deeply. She recalled that on the day before the attack, Tio preached during the Sunday morning service from Job 1:21, "The LORD gave and the LORD has taken away; blessed be the name of the LORD." She marvels that God was preparing her heart for "such a time as this." Sara shared how the Lord had given her many wonderful years with her husband. She understood, "It is God's right to take my husband when and where He wants." Her husband had been a godly man and remained faithful until death. Now Tio is in the presence of our loving, sovereign Lord, and he has received a crown of life. (Revelation 2:10) Sara longs to join her husband one day and even though her pain is great, God has given her peace.

"Sara, are you able to forgive the Muslims for the murder of your husband?" I asked. A sweet, gentle smile came over her face, as she replied, "my husband forgave them, didn't he? Certainly, I can forgive them too, can't I?" Her tender eyes twinkled with God's love.

What motivated these Muslim martyrs to destroy Sara and Tio's home, burn their Church building to the ground, and then purposefully murder Tio while giving praise, honor and sacrificial tribute to Allah the God of the Qur'an?

The Qur'an demands Muslims follow the "pillars of Islam" with reverence, fear, and awe. However, extreme love, Biblical love, conquers the extreme violence within Islam. As extreme love is exemplified in the lives of the Christian believers, there is hope in conquering today's Islamic terrorism. The Christian believer is the vehicle which God has sovereignly designed to accomplish His purpose of implementing this extreme love to the world. Muslims understand martyrdom and the "call" to living a disciplined life. As the Christian believer "lays down his life," then Muslims, as well as unbelievers, will experience God's extreme love first hand. "Loving our enemies" is a radical call that enables and empowers Christians to tangibly express the love and forgiveness of Jesus Christ.

### Fearless Love: Meditation

Jesus wants his disciples to have a great love life. John 13:35 states, "By this all men will know that you are My disciples, if you have love for one another." Tio's immediate reaction was to protect the Church and forgive his enemies. Sara worshipped the Lord that night and called Him blessed. She also forgave.

Righteousness and love come from an intimate relationship with God. How is your love life? Are there areas that you are lacking in love for others and especially your enemies? Thank God that now you know where God wants to enlarge His love in your life. In his last breath Tio prayed for his murderer.

Pray right now that God will use this book to increase your love. Today begin to pray for your enemies. Pray for Muslims. If you find this hard, don't worry. You are not alone! Ask the Lord to help you learn how to pray and love your enemies. Our prayer for you is that you will grow in your intimacy with Him as you read this book.

*Fearless Love Notes:*

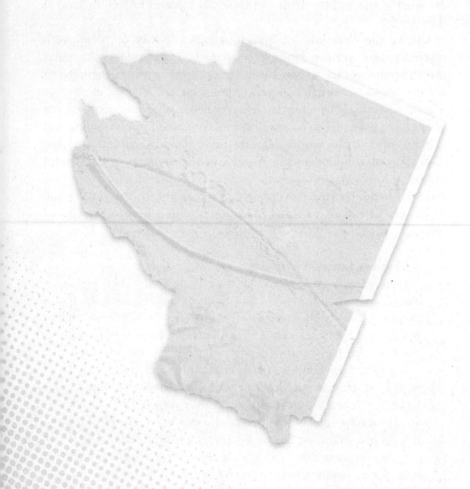

# JIHAD-
## The Great Commission

> The Qur'an is the supreme
> authority within Islam.

I (Mujahid) want to thank Daniel Scot who is a personal friend. The majority of the material from Chapter Two to Chapter Five has been gleaned from his excellent book "Understanding Islam: Analyzing the Qur'an, Hadith and Life of Muhammad" by Daniel Scot. Published by Ibrahim Ministries International, Brisbane Australia. 2005.

Most of the Qur'anic verses are taken from the Pickthall's translation, unless stated otherwise. Note that verse number varies in different Qur'anic translations and editions of the Qur'an.

Muslims have a great commission to spread the teachings of Islam throughout the world. Jihad is the great commission of Islam. Jihad is taught in their holy books, the Qur'an and in the traditions the Hadith. The Qur'an is the supreme authority within Islam. The Qur'an is believed to be the precise words of Allah, given by the angel Gabriel, to the prophet Muhammad. The Hadith are collections of the traditions, practices, and duties that Muhammad approved, including stories of the life of Muhammad written by his disciples.

According to the Dictionary of Islam: "Jihad: An effort, or a striving. A religious war with those who are unbelievers in the mission of Muhammad. It is an incumbent religious duty, established in the Qur'an and in the Traditions as a divine institution, and enjoined specially for the purpose of advancing Islam and of repelling evil from Muslims. When an infidel's country is conquered by a Muslim ruler, its inhabitants are offered three alternatives:

1. The reception of Islam, in which case the conquered become enfranchised citizens of the Muslim states.
2. The payment of a poll-tax (Jizyah), by which unbelievers in Islam obtain protection, and became second class citizens.
3. Death by the sword, to those who will not pay the poll tax."[i]

The Noble Qur'an Surah 2:190 footnote defines jihad with the following: "Al-Jihad (holy fighting) in Allah's Cause (with full force of numbers and weaponry) is given the utmost importance in Islam and is one of its pillars (on which it stands). *By Jihad, Islam is established, Allah's Word is made superior, and His religion (Islam) is propagated.* By abandoning Jihad (may Allah protect us from that) Islam is destroyed and the Muslims fall into an inferior position; their honor is lost, their lands are stolen, their rule and authority vanished. Jihad is an obligatory duty in Islam on every Muslim, and he who tries to escape from this duty, or does not in his innermost heart wish to fulfill this duty, dies with one of the qualities of a hypocrite."[ii]

How many Muslims around the world, in the United States of America, and in your community are in jihad? All of them who believe in the teachings of the Qur'an, and Hadith! "Jihad is an obligatory duty in Islam on every Muslim." The Noble Qur'an also illustrates three important points of jihad;

1. Jihad is the vehicle in which Islam is established.
2. The Qur'an (Allah's Word) is made superior.
3. It is Islam's Great Commission (Islam is propagated).

While the Qur'an and the Hadith specifically teach jihad as a Holy War against infidels, Islamic theologians have developed a doctrine of jihad into four major areas of life.

1. Jihad is an inward spiritual struggle for purity.
2. Jihad is against Satan and the ways he deceives people into idolatry. (Islam is Monotheistic, there is only one God-Allah.)
3. Jihad is against infidels and specifically Jews and Christians who do not submit to Islam.
4. Jihad is against the hypocrites. (Muslims who pretend to practice Islam, but do not follow the precepts of the Qur'an.)

The Qur'an teaches that the religion of Islam should prevail over all religions. Surah 48:28-29: "He it is Who has sent His Messenger (Muhammad) with guidance and the religion of truth (Islam), that He may make it (Islam) superior to all religions…"[iii] Surah 8:39 commands Muslims to fight (katal) until all people become Muslim: "And fight them until there is no more Fitnah (disbelief and polytheism, i.e. worshipping others besides Allah)."[iv]

## Jihad Is Compulsory

The Qur'an declares that there is no reasonable excuse to avoid jihad. Any Muslim who is physically capable of striving in jihad must do so. True Muslims do not avoid jihad as declared in Surah 49:15: "Only those are the believers who have believed in Allah and His Messenger, and afterward doubt not but strive with their wealth and their lives for the Cause of Allah. Those! They are the truthful."

There are some intellectual and liberal Muslims today who try to argue against the physical warfare of jihad. During Muhammad's day there were also "liberal" or "moderate" Muslims who did not desire to fight in jihad and wanted to personally avoid warfare. The Qur'an specifically commands warfare for Muslims. For instance, in Surah 2:216: "Jihad (holy fighting in Allah's Cause) is ordained for you (Muslims) though you dislike it."*v*

Surah 8:67: "It is not for a Prophet that he should have prisoners of war (and free them with ransom) until he had made a great slaughter (among his enemies) in the land." In other words, do not desire this world's comfort before you desire obedience to Allah and jihad. This verse also points out that slaughter must come before captives. Therefore, warfare must come before victory. Victory by peaceful persuasion is not an option.

During Muhammad's day there were Muslims making excuses for not wanting to fight in jihad. One of the excuses was their desire to stay at home with their wives. However, Surah 9:86-87*vi* refutes this excuse.

Other Muslims who were rich complained that the distance to fight was too far and that they should send others to fight. Surah 9:41-42*vii* gives correction to this misguided temptation to avoid jihad because of distance.

Arabia is a very hot place especially during the summer months. Some Muslims wanted to avoid jihad because of the heat of the desert Surah 9:81 counters with these words, "...they said: 'March not forth in the heat.' Say: 'The fire of Hell is more intense in heat...'"

Even religious duty of prayers and charity take second place to jihad as ordered in Surah 4:77-78.*viii*

To delay jihad is not allowed as recorded in the Hadith. "On the day of the conquest of Mecca, the Prophet said...whenever you are called for Jihad, you should go immediately."*ix*

## Jihad-Supreme In Islam

The Noble Qur'an, declares in Appendix III that The Call to Jihad, is ordained and to be pursued with the heart (intentions or feelings) and with the hand (weapons, etc.) and with the tongue (speeches, etc.). In other words, Muslims should love jihad with their heart, hands and tongue.x

### Fearless Love: Meditation

The ultimate obedience within Islam is jihad. By jihad Muslims work off bad deeds and earn favor from Allah for eternal life. What are you "striving" for today? Believers in Christ Jesus have been forgiven and cleansed from their sins. The children of God are to rest in the completed work of Jesus Christ for their righteousness. Romans 8:1 says, "Therefore there is now no condemnation for those who are in Christ Jesus." God's children have present tense forgiveness of their sins so that they can rest. Hebrews 4:10 "For the one who has entered His rest has himself also rested from his works...." If you are weary today from the worries, pain and the sin of this world, seek Jesus. He will give you rest. Jesus desires to bring everyone in this world sweet relief and rest for their souls. Pray that the love of Jesus will touch the weary souls striving in Islam. Pray that God might help you bring them rest as you show them God's love.

### Fearless Love: Endnotes

i    T. P. Hughes, Dictionary of Islam. (Lahore, Pakistan: The Book House Publishers and Booksellers Trust Bldg., Urdu Bazar, Post Box 734 Lahore-2) Pages 243-248.

ii    Dr. Muhammad Taqiuddin Al-Halali and Dr. Muhammad Muhsin Khan, The Noble Qur'an in the English Language, (Riyadh, Saudi Arabia: Darussalam Publishers and Distributors) Page 48.

iii    Pickthall, M. M. The Holy Qur'an. Surah 48:28-29 He it is Who has sent His messenger with the guidance and the religion of truth, that He may cause it to prevail over all religion. And Allah suffices as a Witness. 48:29 Muhammad is the messenger of Allah. And those with him are hard against the disbelievers and merciful among themselves. You (O Muhammad) see them bowing and falling prostrate (in worship), seeking bounty from Allah and (His) acceptance. The mark of them is on their foreheads from the traces of prostration. Such is their likeness in the Torah and their likeness in the Gospel - like as sown corn that sends forth its shoot and strengthens it and rises firm upon its stalk, delighting the sowers - that He may enrage the disbelievers with (the sight of) them. Allah has promised, unto such of them as believe and do good works, forgiveness and immense reward.

iv    Hilali, T. and Khan, M. M. The Noble Qur'an. Surah 8:39 And fight them until there is no more Fitnah (disbelief and polytheism: i.e. worshipping others besides God) and the religion (worship) will all be for God Alone [in the whole of the world]. But if they cease (worshipping others besides God), then certainly, God is All-Seer of what they do.

v    Pickthall, M. M. The Holy Qur'an. Surah 2:216 Warfare is ordained for you, though it is *hateful unto you; but it may happen that you hate a thing which is good for you, and it may happen that you love a thing which is bad for you. Allah knows, you know not.*

vi   Pickthall, M. M. The Holy Qur'an. Surah 9:86 *And when a surah is revealed (which says): Believe in Allah and strive along with His messenger, the men of wealth among them still ask leave of you and say: Suffer us to be with those who sit (at home). 9:87 They are content that they should be with the useless and their hearts are sealed, so that they apprehend not.*

vii   Pickthall, M. M. The Holy Qur'an. Surah 9:41-42 *Go forth, light-armed and heavy-armed, and strive with your wealth and your lives in the way of Allah! That is best for you if you but knew. 9:42 Had it been a near adventure and an easy journey they had followed you, but the distance seemed too far for them. Yet will they swear by Allah (saying): If we had been able we would surely have set out with you. They destroy their souls, and Allah knows that they truly are liars.*

viii   Pickthall, M. M. The Holy Qur'an. Surah 4:77-78. *Have you not seen those unto whom it was said: Withhold your hands, establish worship and pay the poordue, but when fighting was prescribed for them behold! a party of them fear mankind even as their fear of Allah or with greater fear, and say: Our Lord! Why have You ordained fighting for us? If only You would give us respite yet a while! Say (unto them, O Mohammed): The comfort of this world is scant; the Hereafter will be better for him who wards off (evil); and you will not be wronged the down upon a date-stone. 4:78 Wheresoever you may be, death will overtake you, even though you were in lofty towers. Yet if a happy thing befalls them they say: This is from Allah; and if an evil thing befalls them they say: This is of your doing (O Mohammed). Say (unto them): All is from Allah. What is amiss with these people that they come not near to understand a happening?*

ix   Sahih Al-Bukari Hadith Vol. 3, Hadith No. 60 Al-Alim Narrated Ibn Abbas *On the day of the conquest of Mecca, the Prophet said, "There is no more emigration (from Mecca) but Jihad and intentions, and whenever you are called for Jihad, you should go immediately. No doubt, Allah has made this place (Mecca) a sanctuary since the creation of the heavens and the earth and will remain a sanctuary till the Day of Resurrection as Allah has ordained its sanctity. Fighting was not permissible in it for anyone before me, and even for me it was allowed only for a portion of a day. So, it is a sanctuary with Allah's sanctity till the Day of Resurrection.*

x   The Noble Qur'an. Call to Jihad, Page 814, Printed in Saudi Arabia.

*Fearless Love Notes:*

# ISLAM INSTRUCTS
## *Muslims To Fight Until All Their Opponents Submit*

The Qur'an declares how long Muslims must partake in jihad. Muslims must fight non-Muslims until all their opponents submit Surah 9:29: "Fight those who believe not in Allah, nor the last day...until they pay Jizyah {tribute tax- author clarification} with willing submission and feel themselves subdued."*i* Muhammad taught "I have been ordered by (Allah) to fight against the people until they testify that none has the right to be worshipped but Allah, and that Muhammad is his (Allah's) Apostle."*ii*

The Qur'an and Hadith teach that the struggle of jihad will happen until there is worldwide domination and all people everywhere become Muslims.

Presently, the media has picked up on highly publicized beheadings of "infidels" by Muslims. Most people do not understand that these men are simply obeying the Qur'an and offering a sacrifice to the "Cause" of Allah. Surah 47:4: "So, when you meet (in fight-Jihad in Allah's Cause) those who disbelieve, smite (their) necks till when you have killed and wounded many of them, then bind a bond firmly..." Muslims are commanded to behead the unbelievers until the remaining unbelievers are thoroughly subdued. The beheadings of their enemies are a type of religious sacrament when Muslims offer to Allah the heads of "infidels." The beheading videos on the Internet, show the Muslim captors chanting Qur'anic verses and giving instructions to other Muslims on how they are to behead "infidels" in proper "Halal" (Holy) manner, which is acceptable to Allah.

### Judgment Day

"Allah's Messenger said, 'The Hour will not be established until you fight against the Jews, and the stone behind which a Jew will be hiding will say, O Muslim! There is a Jew hiding behind me, so kill him.'"*iii* Islam teaches that a day is coming when all Muslims will rise up against the infidels. Non-believers of Islam will be given one last chance to confess that there is no other god but Allah and His prophet is Muhammad. All those who do not become Muslim on that day will be slaughtered in a great worldwide judgment. This will happen in one event because Allah will perform a miracle. Many Jews and Christians will escape to

According to the Qur'an and Hadith, Jesus will return on judgment day to lead all Muslims in a slaughter of Christians.

the woods and rocks to avoid the slaughter but Allah will give mouths to the rocks and trees which will call out to the Muslims to come and find the Jew or Christian hiding behind them.

According to the Qur'an and Hadith, Jesus will return on judgment day to lead all Muslims in a slaughter of Christians. "And on the Day of Resurrection, he (Isa - Jesus) will be a witness against them." (Surah 4:159)iv As Jesus is leading Muslims in this great slaughter he breaks crosses (a symbol of idolatry according to Islam) and brings vengeance against the Christians for believing that He was the Son of God and that He died for their sins on the cross. "Isa (Jesus), Son of Maryam (Mary) will shortly descend amongst you (Muslims), and will judge mankind justly by the law of the Qur'an (as a just ruler); he will break the Cross and kill pigs and there will be no Jizyah.v (In other words the Muslim Jesus will not accept any Jizyah or Protection money as Mohammad did to the Jews and Christians.)"

Muhammad offered three options:
a. Accept Islam;
b. Pay jiziya – protection money and utterly submit;
c. Jihad (death to the infidel).

The Qur'anic Jesus will only offer two options:
a. accept Islam;
b. Jihad.(death)

Jesus of the Qur'an is a Muslim prophet who brings warning of Allah's judgment against Christians and will one day carry out Allah's wrath against Christians by leading other Muslims in their destruction.

**Two Houses Of Islam**
In the Qur'an there are two groups in which all people are identified.

The first group is called Dar Islam, translated "House of Islam." If you are a Muslim then you are in the House of Islam. Also in this category are countries where Muslims are in the majority and Islamic law (Sharia law) has been established (Saudi Arabia, Iran, etc.).

The second group in Islam is called Dar Harb, translated "House at War". All non-Muslims or hypocrites (moderate or liberal Muslims who are not following the commands of Allah as written in the Qur'an and Hadith) are of the House of War and Muslims must be in jihad against them. The House of War then is in greater context in those countries where Muslims are in the minority and Islamic law has not been established such as Britain, Canada, Germany and the United States. In the Qur'an and Hadith every Muslim is taught that it is his/her duty to bring Islam to these countries by all means.

### Jihad As Self-defense

The Qur'an lists various reasons why jihad is permissible for Muslims when defending themselves. In Surah 2:190*vi* Muslims are instructed to fight infidels who fight against Muslims; "And fight in the way of Allah those who fight you..."

The Qur'an declares that if a Muslim has been wronged then they are free to pursue jihad. Surah 22:39: "Permission to fight (against disbelievers) is given to those (believers) who are fought against, because they have been wronged."

Jihad is justified in the protection of Churches, Synagogues and Mosques as stated in Surah 22:40.*vii* However, when Muhammad had conquered the whole of Arabia, none of the churches or Synagogues could survive. As Muslims captured more lands Christians and Jews were subjugated to Islamic rule. As long as the Christians and Jews submitted to the Islamic rule and paid a tribute tax they were allowed to practice their faith within the confines of the Islamic rulers. Therefore, Muslims became their protectors and were to protect the Churches and Synagogues within their rule against foreign invasions, however jihad could be invoked if any Christians and Jews did not obey the pact of Omar.*viii*

Jihad is justified in the defense for the feeble men, the women and the children. Surah 4:75: "And what is wrong with you that you fight not in the Cause of God, and for those weak, ill-treated and oppressed among men, women, and children, whose cry is: Our Lord! Rescue us from this town whose people are oppressors; and raise for us from You one who will protect, and raise for us from You one who will help."*ix*

## Part One: Chapter 3

Muslims can say that they being oppressed by Western nations because they are forbidden to practice what Allah commands them to do such as:

a. practice polygamy;
b. keeping slaves and
c. beating wives.

### Jihad For Advancement Of Islam

Not only is jihad justified for defensive purposes but it is also commanded for offensive reasons for the spread of Islam.

One clear purpose of offensive jihad in the Qur'an is for economic gain. Surah 48:18-20x tells us that jihad brings economic blessing from Allah from the spoils of the war. "Allah has promised you abundant spoils that you will capture..."

During Muhammad's day most all the other warlords demanded twenty five percent of all the war booty captured during battles and raids. Muhammad offered a better deal of only twenty percent of all booty devoted to Allah Muhammad and the needy. (Surah 8:41)xi This incentive attracted many men to fight on behalf of Allah and Muhammad and many Arabs forsook their previous warlords for economic gain.

Also, during Muhammad's day Arabian tribes would attack each other. The Qur'an offered economic security in forbidding Muslims to attack each other. Therefore, looting of Muslims by other Muslims was strongly discouraged in Surah 4:94.xii This divine protection of Muslims by the Qur'an helped further the Kingdom of Islam. As more and more areas were conquered, Muslims had to travel further to attack infidels for spoils and booty.

Jihad advances Islam when calling Muslims to fight against idolatry. Surah 9:5.13xiii "Then when the Sacred months... have passed, then kill the Mushrikun." Mushrikun is an Arabic word for unbeliever or idol worshipper and those who associate anyone with Allah) Jihad against idolaters specifically targets Jews and Christians. Surah 4:51-52: "Have you not seen those who were given a portion of Scripture... They are those whom Allah has cursed..."xiv

Jihad advances Islam by commanding Muslims to disobey non-Muslim governments. (Surah 25:52xv; Surah 26:151xvi)

We have shown how the Qur'an sets forth jihad for all Muslims everywhere at all times until Islam achieves world domination. Jihad is both defensive and offensive. Today we have millions of Muslims living in countries that are in Houses of War. Nations like the United States of America, England, Germany, India and others. Every Muslim in these nations will admit they are in jihad although they will most often claim that they are "striving" for self-betterment or the betterment of society in manners of peace because they claim Islam is a better system. But the fact of the matter is that the Qur'an commands not to strive for peace but the establishment of Islam in every nation and upon every person. Only when Islam is dominant around the world does Islam teach that there can be peace.

Since Islam's foundation, it has established for Muslims to fight in jihad. The Qur'an and Muhammad declare that judgment day is coming when there will be a massacre of all infidels, with this consistent theme throughout Islam we begin to understand the driving violent spirit that propagates Islam around the world and in which fundamental Muslims continue to promote. Fundamental Muslims see violence as essential in bringing the glory of Islam to fruition.

### Fearless Love: Meditation

Judgment day for Islam is a day when every true Muslim will obey Allah and bring slaughter to their enemies. The Qur'an demanded violence from the beginning days of Islam. Islam has expanded its Kingdom through violence. The domination of Islam will come through a massacre of all non-believers.

The Bible says in Galatians 6:7: "Do not be deceived, God is not mocked; for whatever a man sows, this he will also reap." If Islam were to conquer the world the Bible gives us insight that Muslims would turn against each other. Bloodshed and murder would not cease with the annihilation of their enemies. The Bible tells us the end of the story and that Islam will not rule the earth. Jesus Christ will make a new heaven and new earth. The desire for sin will be abolished and every tear wiped away. Apple seeds produce apple trees. Orange seeds produce orange trees. From the actions of violence come a spirit of violence and thus are the seeds for more violence. The actions of love come from a spirit of love and they are seeds to the human heart to produce a harvest of good. God has given His Spirit to His children and called them to be farmers of love. What seeds are you planting today? Pray that God might plant His Spirit of love in your heart.

# Part One: Chapter 3

## Fearless Love: Endnotes

i   Hilali, T. and Khan, M. M. The Noble Qur'an. Surah 9:29 Fight against those who (1) believe not in God, (2) nor in the Last Day, (3) nor forbid that which has been forbidden by God and His Messenger (4) and those who acknowledge not the religion of truth (i.e. Islâm) among the people of the Scripture (Jews and Christians), until they pay the Jizyah with willing submission, and feel themselves subdued.

Pickthall, M. M. The Holy Qur'an. Surah 9:29 Fight against such of those who have been given the Scripture as believe not in Allah nor the Last Day, and forbid not that which Allah has forbidden by His messenger, and follow not the Religion of Truth, until they pay the tribute readily, being brought low.

ii   Sahih Al Bukhari Vol 1 Hadith Number 24 Allah's Apostle said, "I have been ordered by (Allah) to fight against the people until they testify that none has the right to be worshipped but Allah, and that Muhammad is his Allah's Apostle, and offer the prayers perfectly and give the obligatory charity, so if they perform that they save their lives and property from me."

iii   Sahih Al-Bukhari, Vol. 4. Hadith No. 176, 177.

iv   Pickthall, M. M. The Holy Qur'an. Surah 4:159 There is not one of the People of the Scripture but will believe in him before his death, and on the Day of Resurrection he will be a witness against them.

v   Sahih Al-Bukhari. Vol. 3, Hadith No. 425 Allah's Apostle said, "By Him in Whose Hands my soul is, son of Mary (Jesus) will shortly descend amongst you people (Muslims) as a just ruler and will break the cross and kill the pig and abolish the Jizya (a tax taken from the non-Muslims who are in the protection of the Muslim government). Then there will be abundance of money and nobody will accept charitable gifts.

Sahih Al-Bukhari. Vol. 3, Hadith No. 656 Allah's Apostle said, "The Hour will not be established until the son of Mary (i.e. Jesus) descends amongst you as a just ruler, he will break the cross, kill the pigs, and abolish the Jizya tax. Money will be in abundance so that nobody will accept it (as charitable gifts)."

vi   Pickthall, M. M. The Holy Qur'an. Surah 2:190 Fight in the way of Allah against those who fight against you, but begin not hostilities. Lo! Allah loves not aggressors.

vii   Hilali, T. and Khan, M. M. The Noble Qur'an. Surah 22:40 Those who have been expelled from their homes unjustly only because they said: "Our Lord is God." -- For had it not been that God checks one set of people by means of another, monasteries, churches, synagogues, and mosques, wherein the Name of God is mentioned much would surely have been pulled down. Verily, God will help those who help His (Cause). Truly, God is All-Strong, All-Mighty.

viii   The Pact of Umar is particularly significant because apart from the Qur'an (Sura 9: 28-30), it is the main source of law regarding dhimmis. The Pact has been attributed to Umar I, the second successor of Muhammad (ruled 634-644 AD), or to the Umayyad Caliph Umar II (ruled 717-720 AD) or to a date around 1100 AD during the Abbasid dynasty. However, Ibn Kathir a classic Muslim scholar from 14th century commenting on Sura 9:29, states that the Pact of Umar was imposed by the second caliph (AD 634-646).

Under the Pact of Umar, Jews and Christians made the following undertakings:

We will neither erect in our areas a monastery, church, or a sanctuary for a monk, nor restore any place of worship that needs restoration nor use any of them for the purpose of enmity against Muslims;

We will not prevent any Muslim from resting in our churches whether they come by day or night, and we will open the doors [of our houses of worship] for the wayfarer and passerby. Those Muslims, who come as guests, will enjoy boarding and food for three days;

We will not allow a spy against Muslims into our churches and homes or hide deceit (or betrayal) *against Muslims;*

*We will not teach our children the Qur'an, publicise practices of Shirk (associating anything with Allah), invite anyone to Shirk [to become a Christian] or prevent any of our fellows from embracing Islam, if they choose to do so;*

*We will respect Muslims, move from the places we sit in if they choose to sit in them. We will not imitate their clothing, caps, turbans, sandals, hairstyles, speech, nicknames and title names, or ride on saddles, hang swords on the shoulders, collect weapons of any kind or carry these weapons;*

*We will not encrypt our stamps in Arabic, or sell liquor. We will have the front of our hair cut, wear our customary clothes wherever we are, wear belts around our waist, refrain from erecting crosses on the outside of our churches and demonstrating them and our books in public in Muslim fairways and markets;*

*We will not sound the bells in our churches, except discretely, or raise our voices while reciting our holy books inside our churches in the presence of Muslims, nor raise our voices [with prayer] at our funerals, or light torches in funeral processions in the fairways of Muslims, or their markets;*

*We will not bury our dead next to Muslim dead, or buy servants who were captured by Muslims;*

*We will be guides for Muslims and refrain from breaching their privacy in their homes;*

*We will not beat any Muslim;*

*These are the conditions that we set against ourselves and followers of our religion in return for safety and protection. If we break any of these promises that we set for your benefit against ourselves, then our Dhimmah (promise of protection) is broken and you are allowed to do with us what you are allowed of people of defiance and rebellion. [Ibn Kathir. Tafsir Ibn Kathir. [Abridged] Volume 4. Darussalam, Riyadh. 2000. pp.406-407]. Emphasis added.*

*The only rights one may enjoy are those recognised in the charter and, even then, only for as long as the charter remains valid or as long as those who set its terms deem it still appropriate. The dhimmis if fail to observe the 'Pact' Jihad could be invoked and the dhimmis could be killed at any stage. This, then, is the dhimmi's condition and has not varied throughout history. Furthermore, this is not the result of social chance, but a concept rooted in the very teachings of Islam.*

ix    *Hilali, T. and Khan, M. M. The Noble Qur'an. Surah* 4:75.

x    *Hilali, T. and Khan, M. M. The Noble Qur'an. Surah* 48:18-20 *Indeed, God was pleased with the believers when they gave their Bai'â (pledge) to you (O Muhammad) under the tree, He knew what was in their hearts, and He sent down As-Sakinah (calmness and tranquillity) upon them, and He rewarded them with a near victory, And abundant spoils that they will capture. And God is Ever All-Mighty, All-Wise. God has promised you abundant spoils that you will capture, and He has hastened for you this, and He has restrained the hands of men from you, that it may be a sign for the believers, and that He may guide you to a Straight Path.*

xi    *Hilali, T. and Khan, M. M. The Noble Qur'an. Surah* 8:41 *And know that whatever of war-booty that you may gain, verily one-fifth (1/5th) of it is assigned to God, and to the Messenger, and to the near relatives [of the Messenger (Muhammad)], (and also) the orphans, Al-Masâkin (the poor) and the wayfarer, if you have believed in God and in that which We sent down to Our slave (Muhammad) on the Day of criterion (between right and wrong), the Day when the two forces met (the battle of Badr) -- And God is Able to do all things.*

xii    *Pickthall, M. M. The Holy Qur'an. Surah* 4:94 *O you who believe! When you go forth (to fight) in the way of Allah, be careful to discriminate, and say not unto one who offers you peace: "You are not a believer," seeking the chance profits of this life (so that you may despoil him). With Allah are plenteous spoils. Even thus (as he now is) were you before; but Allah has since then been gracious unto you. Therefore take care to discriminate. Allah is ever Informed of what you do.*

xiii    *Hilali, T. and Khan, M. M. The Noble Qur'an. Surah* 9:5 *Then when the Sacred Months (the 1st, 7th, 11th, and 12th months of the Islâmic calendar) have passed, then kill the Mushrikûn (see V.2:105) wherever you find them, and capture them and besiege them, and prepare for them each and every ambush. But if they repent and perform As-Salât (Iqâmat-as-Salât), and give Zakât, then leave their way free. Verily, God is Oft-Forgiving, Most Merciful.*

xiv   Hilali, T. and Khan, M. M. *The Noble Qur'an. Surah* 4:51-52.

xv   Hilali, T. and Khan, M. M. *The Noble Qur'an. Surah* 25:52 *So obey not the disbelievers, but strive against them (by preaching) with the utmost endeavour, with it (the Qur'ân).*

xvi   Hilali, T. and Khan, M. M. *The Noble Qur'an. Surah* 26:151 . *"And follow not the command of Al-Musrifûn [i.e. their chiefs, leaders who were polytheists, criminals and sinners],*

*Fearless Love Notes:*

*Fearless Love Notes:*

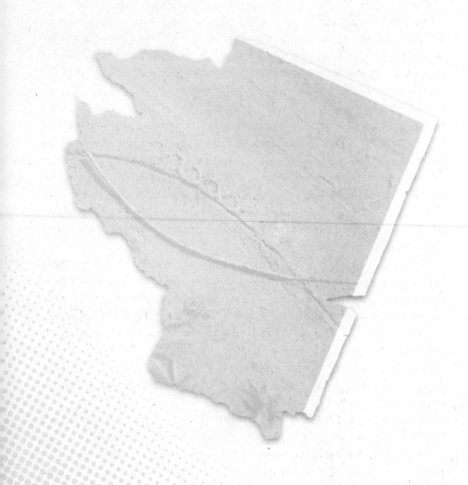

# SILENT
## *Jihad*

Jihad also includes commands for Muslims to advance Islam in ways that are not violent although aggressive and subtle. The subtle commands of Islam are called silent jihad. For the first ten years of Muhammad's ministry he preached and received Qur'anic verses regarding Monotheistic Islamic worship. During this time of his life he spoke a few verses of respect and co-existence of other people of faith. At the most he had 200 converts to Islam during this decade. At the end of ten years he had his revelation of jihad and began to teach that Muslims must resist and fight against infidels. The reasoning was that the non-believers had been warned by the prophet Muhammad and they had resisted. Muslims were called to fight until the infidels submitted either by conversion, tribute, or death. The last 12 years of Muhammad's life he received the Qur'anic verses calling for violent jihad. Today if you read the Qur'an there are a few verses that call for respect and forgiveness of the infidels. However, there are many verses that call for death and fighting against the infidels.

How do Muslim theologians reconcile the difference since there are direct contradictions? Within Islam the doctrine of abrogation was developed. When Qur'anic verses contradicted each other the later verse canceled out any proceeding verses. This doctrine is based on Surah 2:106: "Whatever a Verse (revelation) do We abrogate or cause to be forgotten, we bring a better one or similar to it. Know you not that Allah is Able to do all things?" This verse simply says that Allah changes his mind. The latest revelation of Allah becomes the final authority in any contradiction.

So which verses come last in the Qur'an, the verses that speak of respect for non-Muslims, or the verses about fighting non-Muslims? Fighting non-Muslims was the later revelation of Allah in the Qur'an, consequently, jihad verses supersede all verses regarding mercy and tolerance toward non-believers. Therefore, all the verses within the Qur'an that speak of peace, respect or forgiveness of infidels have been canceled. But those verses are still quoted today from fundamental Muslims as a type of silent jihad or deception. These verses are used as tools of appeasement and propaganda to produce a facade of peace within Islam toward non-Muslims. In other words, historically when Muslims are in the minority they are in what is called silent jihad. Silent jihad is the means by which Muslims who are in the minority strive to propagate Islam in quiet and nonviolent ways. Of course many moderate and liberal Muslims want to believe the authenticity of these verses of peace in hopes of bringing tranquility to Islam. Fundamentalist use the arguments of moderate and liberal Muslims within their silent jihad doctrine to buy time.

In silent jihad we can see a pattern of nine M's: Moral Dilemma, Merchant, Marriage, Money, Mosque, Madarrassa (Islamic training school), Media, Mysticism, and Migration.

### Moral Dilemma

The Qur'an gives religious justification for lying. This is silent jihad by moral dilemma. On one side Muslims desire honesty but for reasons of jihad they are called to lie. Muslims are allowed to lie when they are in danger. Surah 16:106: "Whoever disbelieved in Allah after his belief, except him who is forced...is at rest with Faith" The Qur'an calls for faithful proclamation of belief as a Muslim except him who is forced. Islam allows for deception when Muslims livelihood is at stake. Deception is used as a tool of silent jihad in the propagation of Islam

The Qur'an goes on further to declare that Muslims are not bound by their oaths. Surah 66:2 i) "Allah has already ordained for you, (O men), the absolution of your oaths." Contracts then are only used as a device of silent jihad to buy time so as to attack infidels at a later date and more favorable time.

### Merchant

Muslims are to use their businesses in the striving and propagation of Islam. As I have travelled the world I have met Christians who have told me that their Muslim employer offered them a pay raise and promotion if they would convert to Islam. Those Muslims may not be willing to fly a plane into the World Trade Center but they are active in silent jihad.

### Marriage

"If we cannot take America by force we will take America by marriage," a quote by a Muslim man married to an American woman. Zennah Ministries works with women in America who have married Muslim men. They estimate that ten thousand American women marry Muslim men every year. Marriage to infidel women is silent jihad.

## Money

Money is the next vehicle of silent jihad. The Qur'an commands the use of wealth for striving against non-Muslims, at least 15 times directly and many more implied. As of July 27, 2007 the Dow Jones Islamic Total index was nearly 19 trillion dollars invested in 2440 number of stocks.*ii* Six percent of the Saudi Arabian budget is designated towards the expansion and propagation of Islam.

## Mosque

Building mosques is another form of silent jihad. Mosques are being built all over the world. Islam teaches that where mosques have been built and Muslims have prayed the area is claimed as Islamic land. There are about 3,000 small and large Islamic centers, mosques, and prayer locations in the US. There are about 200 Muslim schools, about 500 Sunday Islamic schools, and six Islamic schools of Islamic higher learning in America.*iii*

## Madarrassa Islamic Schools

Madarrassa (Islamic training school) are being built all throughout Europe, Americas, Asia, Africa and Australia. The majority of them are funded and supported by Saudi Arabian money and are very conservative Islamic schools. They are teaching jihad and hatred towards Jews and Christians specifically, and infidels generally.

## Media

The growth of pro-Islamic rhetoric in the media may be the most extensive silent jihad from the Muslim community today. In 2003, the Center for Arab Islam Relations abbreviated CAIR, led a campaign to fund 16,000 libraries with pro-Islamic books throughout America. CAIR and many Islamic organizations like them in the West continue to address the public on radio, TV, newspaper, and magazines on the merits and "peace" of Islam. They have tried to redefine jihad in the west as "striving for the betterment of self and society." And lines like "radical Muslims have hijacked the Islamic religion to make it look violent." Any criticism of Islam is immediately attacked as hate crimes. Around the world Muslims are lobbying governments to pass hate crime legislation in an effort to censor critics. Laws have already been passed in Canada and Australia and similar laws are being looked at in Britain and the

# Part One: Chapter 4

USA. In an ironic twist, some Muslims, while claiming freedom and betterment of society, have become a threat to freedom of speech.

## Mysticism

Mysticism within Islam is growing rapidly among those wanting to experience a supernatural or spiritual phenomenon. It is estimated that 70% of Muslims engage in some sort of occultism. Islamic Mysticism is most often connected with the Sufi sect. Sufism sees Islam in more of a metaphysical perspective and practices Islam as a means to experience and draw close to Allah.

## Migration

Last of all, silent jihad is practiced through migration. In the last few years it has been estimated that over 100,000 Muslims have migrated every year from Islamic nations to the United States. The numbers are similar throughout Europe.

While the ultimate end of jihad is always violent, the beginning phases of jihad are subtle. Every devout Muslim is engaged in jihad and must be committed, but to the undiscerning eye the striving of most Muslims in jihad is undetectable.

### Fearless Love: Meditation

If you were a Muslim in what ways would you be practicing silent jihad? In what ways do you practice your personal faith? Disciples of Christ are to propagate their faith by being a witness of Jesus Christ. Acts 22:15 says, "For you will be a witness for Him to all men of what you have seen and heard." True Christians witness to others the forgiveness of God in their lives. How is your witness at work, family, school, with your money, with your tongue? Are you known for God's loving forgiveness to others? Pray that the Holy Spirit of God help you in your silent witness this week.

### Fearless Love: Endnotes

i    Pickthall, M. M. The Holy Qur'an. Surah 66:2 Allah has made lawful for you (Muslims) absolution from your oaths (of such a kind), and Allah is your Protector. He is the Knower, the Wise

ii    http://indexes.dowjones.com/mdsidx/index.cfm?event=showIslamicStats#cmc.

iii    http://www.allied-media.com/AM/AM-profile.htm

*Fearless Love Notes:*

*Fearless Love Notes:*

# JIHAD FOR
*Personal Salvation*

Jihad is an established institution of Islam and to fight in jihad is one of the greatest deeds before Allah. To die in jihad is the greatest reward, bar none. In fact, Islam offers no assurance of salvation apart from being martyred for jihad. Therefore, within Islam martyrdom is the absolute pinnacle of obedience. Martyrdom has the greatest honor and reward.

Muhammad extolled the excellencies of martyrdom, in Sahih Al Bukhari Vol.1 Hadith No. 35. Muhammad says concerning martyrdom and Jihad, "I would have loved to be martyred in Allah's cause and then made alive, and then martyred and then made alive, and then again martyred in his cause." Muhammad emphasized on great joy in martyrdom and sowed his own love for jihad and martyrdom. *i*

Those killed in jihad are not dead, but alive says Surah 2:154: "And say not of those who are killed in the way of Allah: 'They are dead.' Nay, they are living, but you perceive (it) not." (The Noble Qur'an *ii*)

Those killed in jihad find sustenance in the presence of their Lord

**One of the interesting reasons why white women are so revered among Muslim men is that the martyrs of Paradise will have the indulgence of naked white virgin women for eternity.**

Allah and rejoice in their reward Surah 3:169-171: "Think not of those as dead who are killed in the way of Allah. Nay, they are alive, with their Lord, and they have provisions." (The Noble Qur'an)

Those killed in jihad shall be with the prophets and saints Surah 4:69: "And whoso obey Allah and the Messenger (Muhammad) then they will be in the company of…the Prophets…the martyrs, and the righteous. And how excellent these companions are!"

According to the Al-Tirmidhi Hadith 1067, those killed in jihad: Have their abode in Paradise; are preserved from the punishment in the grave; are kept safe from the greatest terror; receive a crown of honor, made of a ruby; shall have seventy-two virgins as their wives; shall be in the company of women and immortal youths (boys); (See also Surah 56:15-18.) shall be able to intercede for seventy of their relatives. *iii*

One of the interesting reasons why white women are so revered among Muslim men is that the martyrs of Paradise will have the indulgence of naked white virgin women for eternity. Surah 52:19,22: "Eat and drink with happiness because of what you used to do. They will recline (with ease) on thrones arranged in ranks. And, we shall marry them to Hur (Fair Females) with wide lovely eyes... And, we shall provide them with fruit and meat such as they desire." Surah 56:31-37: "And by water flowing constantly and fruit in plenty whose supply is not cut off... and on couches or thrones, raised high. Verily we have created them (maidens) of special creation and made them virgins." Surah 78:32-34: "Gardens and vineyards, and young full breasted (mature) maidens of equal age and a full cup (of wine)." (The Noble Qur'an)

Muhammad taught that martyrs die without pain. Al Tirmidhi Hadith No.402 states that Muhammad revealed that the death of martyrs is almost painless. A martyr does not suffer when he is slain any more than one of you suffers from being bitten by an ant. *iv*

### Conclusion

As we have seen from Part One, jihad is the great commission of Islam. Every Muslim is called to practice jihad. Jihad will never stop until there are no more non-Muslims in the world. Jihad is the vision of Islam and a major purpose of all Muslims on Earth. Jihad is the glue that brings Muslims together in defending Islam and expanding Islam. Allah rewards jihad with the highest rewards and jihad has the greatest incentives in the Qur'an. Jihad is the vehicle to spread Islam and is believed to ultimately bring worldwide domination of Islam. Islam teaches that peace can come to the world after worldwide jihad and global domination only. Jihad is the religious justification for the killing and persecution of millions of Christians and other people of faith around the world.

In the following parts we will compare the call of martyrdom in Islam to the call of martyrdom in the Bible. We will show that the call of martyrdom in the Bible is love. This is the question I pray each reader attempts to answer. Which is more powerful? Is martyrdom of violence more powerful than love? Or does the martyrdom of love triumph over violence?

**Fearless Love: Meditation**

God has written his character of love upon all of his creation and people. (Romans 1:19-20) People of all religions and even atheists recognize the greatest gift anyone can give to another is their life. Universally people know that love is never forced. Love gives before it takes. Firefighters, policemen or soldiers who have lost their lives in the line of duty draw the attention of their community. They are heralded as heroes; the community mourns together and gains inspiration. Islamic martyrdom draws its inspiration from the character of God which God has inscribed upon all humankind. That is our lives were designed to be given in worship for a greater purpose.

Unfortunately, Islamic jihad is short sighted and misdirected in calling for lives to be taken in violence when God intended martyrdom for the giving of love and not the taking of life. John 10:17-18 "For this reason the Father loves Me, because I lay down My life so that I may take it again. No one has taken it away from Me, but I lay it down on My own initiative. I have authority to lay it down, and I have authority to take it up again. This commandment I received from My Father." Are you a giver or a taker? Pray that Jesus will give you His authority that you might have the power to give to your enemies. Pray for terrorists to have insight into the deeper meaning of martyrdom which is in giving and not taking.

# Part One: Chapter 5

## Part 1 Group Discussion And Contemplation

Start with prayer for the group to share openly and ask God to give each person greater spiritual insight into Islamic jihad.

*Optional Audio Book: Play Disc 1, Track 13,*
*Jihad for Personal Salvation—for five minutes*

When you think of martyrdom what feelings and associations do you have with that word?

Would you consider Tio a martyr? Why or why not? How does his example inspire you or scare you?

Sara remembered that her husband preached from Job 1:21 the day before his martyrdom. Read Job 1:21 over. Why did this verse bring Sara comfort?

Both Tio and Sara were able to forgive their enemies yet the murderers did not ask for forgiveness. Was this an act of mercy or weakness? Explain your answer.

Tio gave the ultimate sacrifice and Sara forgave them thus they fulfilled the command of love. The Muslim gunman was also obedient to his scriptures in fighting against infidels. Can we judge either party right or wrong for their obedience of faith? (Read Romans 2:15-16.) Which act of obedience was more effective in spreading their faith to others?

The great commandment of Islam is to pursue jihad. The great commandment of the Bible is to love God with all your heart, mind and strength. Which commandment is more powerful in your opinion? Why?

In your opinion, how do most Muslims understand and view Christianity? Do you think that most Muslims know that loving God is the greatest commandment of Christianity and loving others is the second? Why or Why not?

Muslims are commanded to defend and fight for Allah. Why would Allah need to be defended? What does this tell us about the God of Islam? The God of the Bible commands in Romans 12:19, "'VENGEANCE IS MINE, I WILL REPAY,' says the Lord." What do these two commands tell us about the power of Allah of the Qur'an and the power of God of the Bible?

In what ways have you observed silent jihad being practiced? Can you recognize silent jihad in your own community?

If you were a Muslim and only knew of Islam would you be attracted by martyrdom? Why or why not?

Since salvation is so clear for martyrs of Islam what do you think holds more Muslims back today from violent jihad and suicide bombing? Read Romans 2:1-16 and discuss its implications.

Does the media report on the teachings and depth of jihad today? Why or why not? In general do institutional churches teach on jihad of Islam? Why or why not? Should the general public know more about

# Part One: Chapter 5
Islam's teaching on jihad? Why or why not?

Do you think the teaching of jihad is dangerous to worldwide stability and peace today? If so, in what ways?

Many governments are fighting fundamental Muslims that are proclaiming jihad. Many "jihadist" have been killed in the war on terror. What do you think is the attitude of God when a terrorist dies? Ezekiel 18:23 "Do I have any pleasure in the death of the wicked," declares the Lord GOD, "rather than that he should turn from his ways and live?" What is your attitude towards the destruction of the wicked? Pray that God might make your heart and mind more like His.

What hope do Muslims have today? How can you contribute to bringing hope in this world of violence?

**Witness**: This week look for examples of silent jihad. Watch the media and listen well to what you hear and see. Clip out a newspaper or magazine article and share it with others. Look on the internet for examples. Consider what is says and how it lines up with the Qur'an. As you find these examples pray for the media and the world that their eyes are opened to the spiritual battle of the days in which we live. Pray for Muslims worldwide. Pray for Christians worldwide to imitate the life of Christ.

**Personal Application**: In what way has your life helped or hindered the current world wide conflict with Islam? Have you believed and passed on misinformation regarding Islam based upon popular political correctness? Have you slandered Muslims or propagated hateful and vengeful statements? Ask God to help you see the truth of Islam seasoned with His grace.

**Going Deeper:** For more teaching on Islam go to www.fortheloveofmuslims.com and click the link to hear more talks from Dr Mujahid El Masih.

**Ending Prayer**: Pray through the points and insights that you gained.

### Fearless Love: Endnotes

i    Al-Tirmidhi, Hadith 402, The Alim Software, 2001

ii   Hilali, T. and Khan, M. M. The Noble Qur'an

iii  The Alim Software, 2001

iv   Al Tirmidhi Hadith No. 402 The Alim Software, 2001

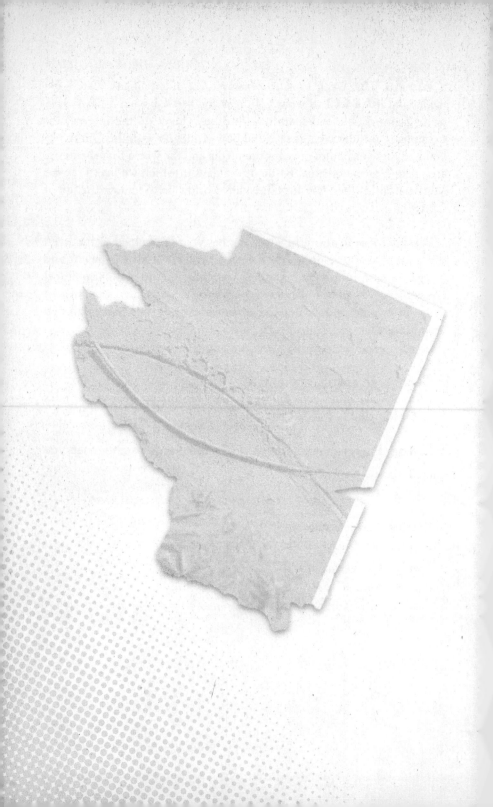

Part Two:

# FROM ASHES TO GLORY

*A Jihadist Changed By Jesus*

*Fearless Love Notes:*

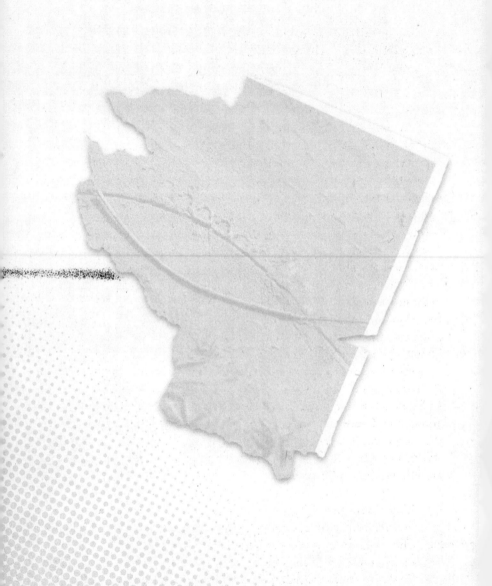

# PAKISTAN - HOMES ON FIRE
## The Story Of Mujahid El Masih

The clock reads just past 8:00 a.m. on February 6, 1997. I have just finished a beautiful time of prayer and breakfast. I walk to the court yard of my host home and feel a refreshing breeze. Quiet fills the air. Suddenly the peace shatters as I hear gun shots and screams of Muslims. Shouts become louder as mobs of angry Muslims race toward our homes and pass on the street calling for the death of Christians. "Burn down their homes and Churches. Allah Akbar," (Allah is Greater) they repeat.

I am not at my home of Shanti Nagar but a few miles away; last night I spent the night at another Church which is also the home of a Christian family. The home is surrounded by a wall and has a court. A Christian man in panic comes through the court gate with his eyes wide with fear. He tells us Shanti Nagar is burning. The town is destroyed. All the Christians are slaughtered! My heart fills with terror and grief. The name Shanti Nagar means "Jerusalem or City of Peace." Our peace is stolen! Our Jerusalem is burning. A scripture comes to my mind. "...The wall of Jerusalem is broken down and its gates are burned with fire. ...when I heard these words, I sat down and wept and mourned for days..." (Nehemiah 1:3b-4a).

*Now I am a martyr of love and the gospel of Jesus Christ*

I peek out into the street and see masses of Muslims in bedlam bringing destruction to Christian homes and businesses. My friend and I are in danger. This Christian worker and I agree to escape through the back wall and go down an alleyway. With chaos increasing in the main street, we discreetly make our way outside the town to a mustard field.

The mustard plant grows as high as seven feet tall in Pakistan. We go to the center of the field and hide among the plants. The pleasant smell of the yellow mustard flower, is a contrast to the smoke of the burning villages. We fall on our knees and begin to pray. The Muslim masses pass on the road just 100 feet from us. We cry out to God, "Lord if today is our day that we must die then help us to be faithful until death. We do not want to deny you!"

The purpose of this chapter is to share my testimony and the journey of how I came to the desire to live for Christ and to die for Christ. My life is representative of the struggle and spiritual development of religious minorities living in Islamic nations. I also can speak for millions of Muslims lost in the Islamic system. I devoted part of my life dedicated to Allah and to strive as a good Muslim. My life started in religious confusion then drifted into a fanatical and a violent desire to die as a Muslim martyr to achieve Islamic glory and Paradise. Finally, I found peace in my heart and purpose in my life by experiencing the grace of Jesus Christ. Now I am a martyr of love and the gospel of Jesus Christ has given me compassion for Muslims.

### Fearless Love: Meditation

Tragedy, suffering and persecution all test our character. Difficulty usually comes suddenly, unexpectedly and jostles' us. Mujahid found himself tested by persecution and cried out to God to be found faithful. The famous Missionary, Amy Carmichael, shared that the jostling of a cup reveals its contents. If the cup contains tea then tea spills out and if milk, milk will splatter. In the same way when a child of Jesus is jostled by suffering the content of his or her character is revealed. If the content of the Christian is love; then love flows, and if it is bitterness; bitterness flows. Persecution and suffering are tools God uses to test us and reveal His witness in us. Luke 8:13 (ESV) says, "And the ones on the rock are those who, when they hear the word, receive it with joy. But these have no root; they believe for a while, and in time of testing fall away." When was the last time you suffered tragedy? What characteristics were revealed in your heart? Thank the Lord for the seeds of righteousness planted in your heart from that day and how much you've changed to spill out compassion and love. Repent of the issues of unrighteousness that God brings to remembrance and allow God to root out bitterness and fill your brokenness with His goodness.

*Fearless Love Notes:*

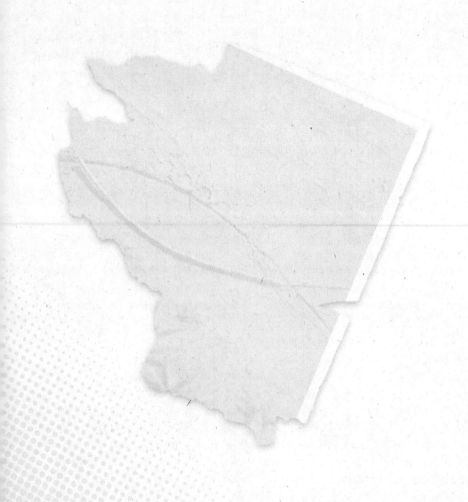

I grew up in a land of religious confusion. Our country is 97% Muslim, 2% Christian, and a mixture of Hindu, Baha'i and many other small religious minorities. Superstition, fear, and division between people abound everywhere. Pakistan is a land of religious adherence, but lacking in love. Poverty is the norm for most of its citizens.

> As I began to hear more and more stories about Muhammad, I found myself attracted to Islam.

My mother birthed eight children but four died in infancy before I was born. My family was a typical nominal Christian family in Pakistan. We were poor, living in a town of other poor Christians. My mother was illiterate and my father had a sixth grade education. My father went to Church on a regular basis but he rarely took the family. He would not pray with us, or read the Bible to us. He belonged to the Pakistani Full Gospel Church. His brother lived next door and was a pastor of the Assembly of God Church. There was tension between the family members because they were involved in different Churches.

Most nights my Uncle had services in his home, only a few feet from our house. We played our music loud to interrupt his services. Hatred and cruelty is such a part of the society in Pakistan that many of the cultural Christians exemplify the same deeds as Muslims. All the sins are the same in our country, but our religions keep us separate and suspicious of each other. The fact is that all Churches, denominations, and religious sects of Islam are divided from the top down and the bottom up. The Bible lists the fruit of the Spirit as "love, joy, peace, patience, kindness, goodness, faithfulness, gentleness, self-control..." But the deeds of the flesh are "...immorality, impurity, sensuality, idolatry, enmities, strife, jealousy, outbursts of anger, disputes, dissensions, factions, envying, drunkenness, carousing, and things like these..." (Galatians 5:19-22). Unfortunately, you can see many deeds of the flesh in Pakistan. But God is redeeming Pakistanis out of this condition. I am one recent example of what God is doing in Pakistan. Please pray for the Churches, Mosques and all the people of Pakistan.

The summer break from school before my sixth grade year began with a Christian outreach team coming to my village to minister. We had a big court yard at our home and we hosted the services every evening. I was attracted by their love and so I volunteered to wait upon them and bring them water and food as they needed it. In the evening, I listened to the gospel presentation and the love and forgiveness of Jesus touched my heart. I prayed to receive Jesus into my heart and promised to follow Him. Joy filled my soul and I was baptized that week. It was a good summer and for the next two months I found myself reading the Bible, praying and attending Church services. I had great zeal but I lacked discipleship and a foundation of Bible knowledge.

### Islamic Studies

When summer ended, I started my sixth grade year. My teacher was a very cruel man. He was a devout Muslim and forced the students to memorize parts of the Qur'an. I noticed that he was easier on the Muslim students and they already knew many parts of the Qur'an. The language of the Qur'an is Arabic and foreign to us Christian students so memorization was very difficult. Every day for the first month he beat me with a large stick for not having the memorization of the Qur'an down perfectly. I hated these beatings and I wanted to learn the Qur'an to avoid them. I was told about a Muslim family who would help me memorize the Qur'an. I began to go to their home after school every day to be tutored. Finally my memorization improved and the beatings stopped. I decided to tutor with this family for four months.

As I began to hear more and more stories about Muhammad, I found myself attracted to Islam. To an eleven year old these are exciting stories. My hormones were beginning to change and I was developing an interest in girls. I heard how Muhammad married one of his wives named Aisha when she was only nine years old. Islam seemed to empower me as a boy. I was impressed by Muhammad in how he ruled the people and spoke the words of Allah. Christians are second class citizens, looked down upon and treated with disdain. Muslims in Pakistan have positions of power and are respected. In the midst of all this, Islam seemed to be a superior religion to me.

I decided I must not convert and become a Muslim. It would have brought shame upon my family since we were Christian by religion. But I was no longer interested in my Christian faith so I began to take serious my Islamic studies which I continued for the rest of my school years. In my sixth grade year I was a typical adolescent who was selfish in most of my ways, and I enjoyed the pleasures of the world. I played games with friends, watched movies, and lied when convenient.

I was a very good student at my school and earned top grades. I also had a keen gift in public speaking. A debate was being held at my school and my teacher enrolled me. I competed against all ages. In the final round I faced a young man in college. The judges gave me a higher score and I won the event. All through school I continued to do well and I seemed to have favor with both the students and the teachers.

### Fearless Love: Mediation

Mujahid said, "I grew up in a land of religious confusion." In what way is there religious confusion in your life today? In what way is there religious confusion in society? Humankind and religions have in common spiritual world views to explain life and dictate right and wrong behavior. 1 Corinthians 14:33(ESV) says, "For God is not a God of confusion but of peace." Religion often brings division but Jesus brought peace and love. Consider the words of the Apostle Peter in Acts 10:34-36(GNB): "Peter began to speak: 'I now realize that it is true that God treats everyone on the same basis. Those who fear him and do what is right are acceptable to him, no matter what race they belong to. You know the message he sent to the people of Israel, proclaiming the Good News of peace through Jesus Christ, who is Lord of all.'" If you are not experiencing peace in your life today, ask Jesus Christ to show you His peace and lead you in His love. Pray that your eyes might be open to see the areas the world wishes to bring fear through a spirit of religion instead of a pure love and faith based upon the life of Jesus Christ.

**If you are not experiencing peace in your life today, ask Jesus Christ to show you His peace and lead you in His love**

*Fearless Love Notes:*

# BECOMING
## *a Muslim*

In Pakistan you graduate from High School in the tenth grade. My English teacher helped complete my admissions papers to college. He was a cultural Christian and told me that if I put my given Christian name I would be looked down upon and persecuted. He said I should apply with a Muslim name and I would have a much greater chance to advance through college. At this point I did not have much regard for Christianity. I was attracted by Islam and I had a future to be concerned about so I agreed to his suggestion. I did not share this with my family or Christian community. This began a double life for me. When I was with Muslims I was a Muslim and when I was with Christians I was a Christian. In later years, when my family and friends found that I had changed my name they did not question it because many Christians in Pakistan live this double life to avoid the bigotry and persecution. It is very typical for Christians doing business with Muslims to hide their Christian identity by using Muslim greetings and Muslim names.

I was accepted that fall to college. I studied pre-med and I desired to become a doctor. With a Muslim identity and as a good student I continued to excel in college.

### Ready To Die For Allah

At the same time, I joined the college National Guard Corps because I wanted to learn to fight and shoot a gun. I also knew that if I joined the military after college the government would pay for my medical education. In the National Guard I began indoctrination training in jihad. They taught me that if I died fighting for my country and my religion (Islam), I would go to Paradise. In Paradise I would have seventy-two eternal virgins and unending utopian sex. Please understand that I was in college and my hormones were fully alive. Paradise, full of beautiful

More and more I was attracted to the idea of dying in jihad. In Islam, martyrdom is the only assurance to Paradise.

women at this age was very seductive and I liked the idea. Every day we shouted different Islamic creeds and Qur'anic verses. The cadets heard lectures weekly on military tactics with constant jihad theology intertwined. More and more I was attracted to the idea of dying in jihad. In Islam, martyrdom is the only assurance to Paradise. Through guard training we continued to have a diet of martyrdom. As a Muslim, even if you do the five pillars of Islam you still do not have assurance that you will go to Paradise when you die. I did not participate in Muslim prayer times or go to the Mosque. Neither did I desire to do the Muslim fast during Ramadan or participate in the Hajj and travel to Mecca. I was poor so I did not give alms to the poor. What good would these acts do for me I would reason. I had already seen the hypocrisy of Christians and Muslims. Martyrdom was the eternal trump card and I did not need vain works of religious duty. If I died as a martyr for Allah I could have it all, and I was on my way!

In Islam you are believed to be a Muslim when you repeat the creed which says, "There is no other god but Allah and Muhammad is his prophet." I had a Muslim name, I was saying the creed and other Islamic creeds daily during military drills and I was more committed to dying in jihad than most Muslims. I figured these actions were all that really counted and were most important. Hatred was also growing in my heart. I was taught that India was our number one enemy. Next were the Jews and Israel specifically. The third enemy was America. I was taught to hate them all and that to kill any of them would be a great accomplishment and acceptable to Allah.

After two years of college I graduated with honors. I was accepted to officer training in the Pakistani Military in Karachi, 800 miles away from my home town. The first day at training two soldiers were assigned to me. They were at my command to do whatever I needed. They would shine my shoes, cook a meal or run my errands. I felt powerful. Officer training lasted a month, and I was immersed in military training and jihadist theology. Daily I led men in marches and Islamic chants. Again, I excelled in military training. I studied well and knew my subjects. I was on the verge of a successful military career.

**Fearless Love: Meditation**

Mujahid found that he was living a double life. Christianity was the identity of his childhood. And Islam was the way to achieve his worldly desires. Islam would enable him to achieve status, promotion and material gain in this life and the life to come. He followed whatever idea and identity at any given moment which served his fleshly desires. His belief system was based upon his own selfish gain and not truth outside himself. The fruit of all this was a growing hatred. Have you found yourself living a double life at times? What parts of your belief system are based upon your own gain and comfort and what parts are founded upon the Word of Christ? Matthew 6:24: "No one can serve two masters, for either he will hate the one and love the other, or he will be devoted to the one and despise the other. You cannot serve God and money. Confess in prayer today the areas that you have served another master other than God. Pray for the Christians living in Islamic nations that God strengthen them to flee the temptation to follow Islam and serve another god. Pray that we all grow in unified love.

*Fearless Love Notes:*

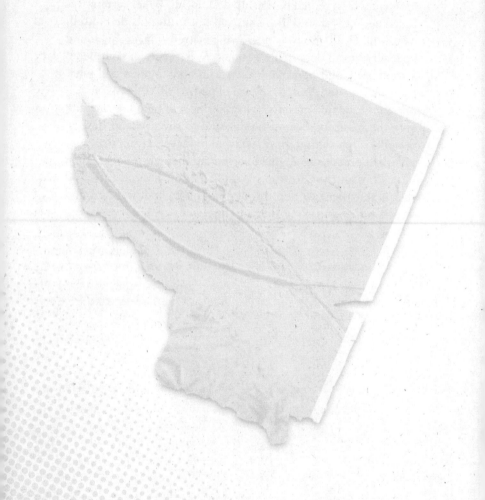

# RUNNING
*From God*

2 Timothy 2:13: "...if we are faithless, he will remain faithful, for he cannot disown himself." Even though I had prayed to receive Christ when I was eleven years old and then walked away from my faith in Jesus by turning to Islam, He had not walked away from me.

The last day of training I had to take an exam. On this morning I was alone in my room as I prepared for the test. All of a sudden I heard an audible voice say, "This job will lead to destruction." At this point, I did not recognize it to be the voice of Jesus but it shook me and I was very disturbed. I prayed that if this is God then he needed to help me get out of the military.

The test for completion of officer training contained 80 questions. I was still quivering in my spirit when I entered the exam room. I knew the questions because I had studied well. The second question was written unclearly so I decided to skip it and come back to it at the end. The answers to the test were on a computerized scan sheet. Little did I know at the time but I began to put each answer in the wrong column. I answered question three in column two then for answer four I put in column three and so forth. I ran out of time right as I finished the 80th question and did not have time to go over my test. Consequently, I failed my military exam and I was dismissed from the military life.

From 1989-1990 I studied two years at the University of Multan in Chemistry. I still desired to fight for the military. I tried to put the voice of God out of my mind. Things about military life were very attractive: Paradise for martyrs; the respect of others; a good salary; good housing and a special school for military children. I hoped to be accepted back into the military but God did not let this happen.

In Karachi, I found a teaching job at an Islamic High School. I was a man without peace and desperation filled my soul. I only taught for six months. Then I took another teaching position, again I quit and found another school. I changed teaching jobs four times and finally decided teaching was not for me.

I enjoyed playing music and I began performing with a musical group as a singer. We quickly became popular and kept busy playing for weddings, parties and religious events. One day I sang at a Muslim shrine for a religious ceremony. People were giving tribute to a religious spiritual leader who they believed had many powers. This man was casting out demons and sending the demons to other people. As I sang they washed the feet of this Islamic priest. The water was black with filth and grime. The people believed this water was holy and blessed because it came from the spiritual leader. They drank the dirty water and washed their faces and bodies. The atmosphere was thick in a way that made my skin crawl. While I sang and observed this demonic worship the same voice I had heard three years before spoke to me. The voice told me that I should immediately leave; that if I kept playing my life would be destroyed. I finished the song and told the band that I was done and needed to leave. We were being paid well and the band wanted me to come back the next day. I told everyone that I was through.

I moved back to my home village. My soul was dark with hatred. At one point, I found out that a local family was stealing water from our small farm. I plotted to kill the whole family. I hid near the spot where they were stealing with a gun in hand. That day they did not come. I now know that God protected me, for I would have been put into prison for their murder. This incident was just another example of the rage that was in my heart.

I was a man wandering and my life was without peace. In my home village I met Christians who befriended me. They were going on a retreat and asked if I might come along and play music for them. I liked them and decided to go.

## Finding Peace

At the retreat a Pakistani pastor approached me one night. He told me that Jesus could give me peace in my heart if I opened up to His love. The pastor quoted the words of Jesus as recorded in John 14:6: "I am the way, the truth, and the life, and no one shall come to the Father except through me." I was thunderstruck. For the first time in years I now understood that the peace I was looking for was found in Jesus. Jesus died for my sins. He was resurrected and He is alive. The speaker told me that I had one foot in one boat and the other foot in another boat. These were prophetic words. I was barely staying afloat. I was living a double life, having a Christian upbringing and acting as a Christian only when around other Christians, but I had converted to Islam and in my heart I was committed to Jihad. I was selfish, living for myself and inside I felt like an empty shell. The pastor's words pierced the wall over my heart and I cried like a baby as I finally gave my life to Jesus.

This was a glorious night as Jesus became my Savoir and Lord! He once again took my heart and reconciled me with my Heavenly Father. At this point, I had forgotten how to pray but He taught me to pray and gave me the desire to read His Word, the Bible.

I thought back to my studies of Islam and how for a season I trusted the words of Allah and Muhammad but they had not given me peace. Muhammad is dead and Muslims can visit his grave site today. Jesus' grave is empty. Muhammad could not forgive my sins, Jesus forgave my sins. Muhammad said that he could not intercede even for his beloved daughter Fatamah on judgment day. Jesus loved me and is interceding for me before God in Heaven. How could I ever say no to the love of Jesus!

That weekend, understanding and faith filled my heart and mind. I confessed my sin and surrender my life to Christ. Peace filled my soul. I was a new creation and I felt it.

### Fearless Love: Meditation

Peace for most people can be evasive and momentary at best. As we look around the world we find little peace; much war, division, hatred, and discrimination. Families are broken. Many look for peace in beautiful scenery like the mountains or beaches. Some turn to religions. Others find temporary peace in sex, drugs, art and music. The Bible calls Jesus The Prince of Peace.(Isaiah 9:6) Jesus said, "Come to me, all who labor and are heavy laden, and I will give you rest." ( Matthew 11:28) A life at rest is a life of peace. Jesus entered into the heart of Mujahid and brought calm to the furor raging in his heart and mind. Where is your peace today? Invite Christ to come and bring peace to the stormy areas of your life. Pray for others in conflict. Pray for the men and women in terrorist organizations that Jesus bring peace to their conflicted souls so that they might bring God's true peace and love in their community.

*Fearless Love Notes:*

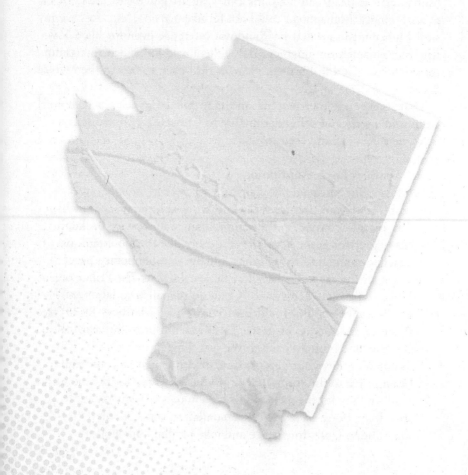

# CALLED
## To Pastor

I had no theological training; I only had a simple faith, and did not know much about my new faith, but I had a great zeal and began to share Christ with others. God worked upon my heart to become a pastor. I did not want to become a pastor because pastors made little money and they were persecuted. But then, at my Church the pastor preached from the book of Jonah. Jonah had a call to preach the Word of God to Nineveh and he tried to avoid this command from God. He ended up being swallowed by a giant fish and spit up near Nineveh and now was ready to obey. I did not like that sermon. God won out and spoke to my heart that He would provide for my life and that I was to trust Christ. I was accepted to a Bible school in Lahore and spent a year and a half there. A scholarship made it possible to complete my Bible training in South Africa.

After this time I became a pastor and went back to my home village of Shanti Nagar. I was very zealous and God was working in mighty, miraculous ways. One day I was riding as a passenger on a motor bike. I passed a Muslim man sitting next to his paralyzed wife on the side of the street. God prompted me to turn around and speak to the man. I asked him, "What is wrong with your wife? And where are you taking her?" He said his wife was paralyzed and he was taking her to a Muslim shrine. He hoped that the Muslim holy man would pray for her and that she would be healed. "Where else have you taken her?" I asked.

He began to name many shrines he had visited but his wife had not been healed. "Have you prayed in the name of Allah?" I ask. He said, "Yes, but it did not work."

"Did you pray in the name of Muhammad?"

"Yes, but she became worse!" He replied.

"Have you heard about Jesus? When He was in this world He healed the sick, raised the dead and made the cripple walk. It is even in the Qur'an. He is alive! Do you want us to pray for your wife in the name of Jesus for her healing?" He said, "Yes!"

Thank God my wife was with me at the time. She laid her hand on the paralyzed woman as I began to cry out loudly in the name of Jesus for his wife to walk. God had already spoken to my heart and I knew God was going to heal her so I prayed loudly to attract others to come and watch the power of God at work. Many people were in the street and a crowd began to form. As we said, "amen" the lady stood up and started to walk. Glory to the Lord Jesus, she was healed. Jesus is still a miracle working God! Many miracles happened during this period of my life. We rejoiced in all that God was doing and we were blessed to help start fourteen house Churches during this first season of my life as a pastor.

### Fearless Love: Meditation

Matthew 14:14 records, "When He went ashore, He saw a large crowd, and felt compassion for them and healed their sick." Jesus heals hurting people because he loves them. He works through His children to pray for the sick and point the way of faith in His name. Mujahid was a vessel of God's healing love to a sick and desperate Muslim couple. Jesus has no obligation to heal anyone. We have sinned. We are unrighteous. Jesus heals simply because he loves us. Sometimes Christ heals the heart to help endure the sickness and sometimes Christ heals the sickness altogether. Are you sick in soul or body today? Bring your pain to Jesus. He promises to have compassion on you and bring you healing.(John 16:24) Pray for the Muslim world today that Jesus bring healing to their ailments, toil and suffering.

Pray for the Muslim world today that Jesus bring healing to their ailments, toil and suffering.

*Fearless Love Notes:*

*Fearless Love Notes:*

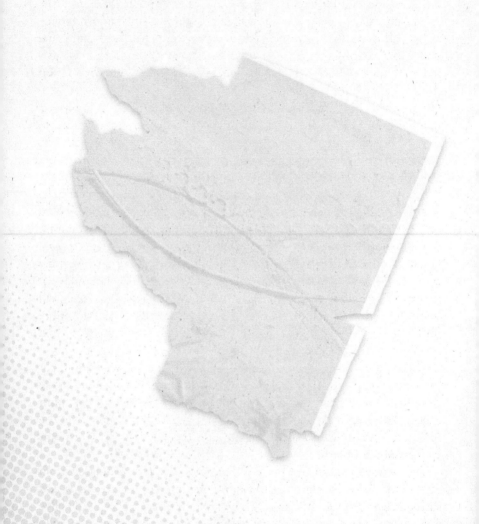

# ATTACK BY
## *Muslim Mobs*

Tension was building between the police in our area and the Christians. A Christian had filed charges against the local police station claiming they had misused their power. He claimed that some police came to his home and during an investigation they threw his Bible to the ground and kicked it. The police wanted the charges dropped and they threatened the Christians with harsh retaliation if the charges were not dropped. The Christian man who brought the charges was a cultural non practicing Christian; he was a hard man, known to be dishonest and rarely in Church. He decided not to drop the charges. The police took action. On the morning of Thursday, February 6, 1997, Christians were falsely accused of tearing the Qur'an and throwing it into the mosque.

February 6th was the last day of Ramadan, the 30 day fast for Muslims. This day is an historical day and many Christians have been persecuted on this day throughout Islamic history. For 30 days Muslims fast during daylight hours. They do not eat, drink or have sexual intimacy. The Qur'an is divided into thirty sections and they read a section every day so that the whole Qur'an is read during Ramadan. The last night of Ramadan is called the night of power when they believe that Allah will hear their prayers and the righteous deeds of Muslims become more powerful on that night. During much of Ramadan Muslims pray and sleep during the day then they eat and gather at night.

Throughout that February night in 1997 the police spread a rumor that the Christians had torn the Qur'an and thrown it into a mosque. Many Muslims were incited to seek revenge on the Christians. That night Muslims rose up from all over the area and began to scream out in the mosque's loud speakers for Muslims to take revenge and kill Christians and burn their homes.

The newspaper articles and reports from that day estimated from 30,000 to 70,000 Muslims rioted against the town of Shanti Nagar and surrounding villages. The line of Muslims marching on the village was five miles long in one direction and a mile long in another direction. Complete chaos was in the streets. Shanti Nagar and surrounding Christian villages were in flames. Cattle and livestock were burned alive. Farms and fields were set on fire. Vehicles were destroyed. The local medical center, the schools and all the Church buildings were burned to the ground.

# Part Two: Chapter 11

Men, women and children were running for their lives. Women who were pregnant were fleeing on foot; some gave birth as they were running. Approximately, two hundred women were raped. It is hard to put into words the depth of our sorrow in the midst of this painful and traumatic event. The babies born had no clothes and were in the cold; approximately one thousand five hundred homes and thirteen Church buildings were burned. We had no home insurance, farm insurance, business insurance or auto insurance. Christians of Shanti Nagar lost everything they had in three hours.

> Love hurts and forgiveness costs a lot... The most expensive gift any child of God has ever received is salvation.

Three days later on Sunday morning 20,000 homeless Christians met in unity for a corporate worship service. As one of the pastors in the area I was asked to speak. I sought the Lord on what to say to these devastated believers. The Holy Spirit led me to speak on forgiveness. The Lord wanted me to remind the Christians that we are to forgive our enemies, the Muslims. "'Vengeance is mine, I will repay,' says the Lord" (Romans 12:19). This is the hardest message I have ever been asked to give. All these Christians have been violated, made homeless and impoverished. Now I am to tell them to forgive the Muslims. God's hand was upon me and the Holy Spirit moved upon the people as I spoke of the power of forgiveness. At the end of my message I asked for all the Christians to stand and pray that they would be able to forgive the Muslims who destroyed their lives. All the people stood and we prayed in unison.

One week later a train full of Muslims derailed and over one hundred Muslims were killed. This happened in the city close to Shanti Nagar. Most of the Muslims had come from that city to attack our village. When the train derailed in this city and Muslims died, many Muslims believed that it was an act of God. A fear of the Christians temporarily descended upon the Muslims bringing some peace.

### Fearless Love: Mediation

Love hurts and forgiveness costs a lot! The Pakistani believers lost all of their earthly belongings and were physically attacked and violated. The most expensive gift any child of God has ever received is salvation. The cost of our sin was Jesus being stripped of his earthly belongings, violated and his blood to be shed. His love is so great for you that He overcame your wrong and forgave you from the cross. That's right! Christ forgave you before you even asked. (Luke 23:34) The Holy Spirit enabled Mujahid and the Pakistani believers to overcome their bitterness and desire for revenge by replacing it with forgiveness. It was not cheap for God to forgive us. It is not easy for us to forgive others but now we have a new covenant from God to give us a way. Matthew 26:28, "... for this is My blood of the covenant, which is poured out for many for forgiveness of sins." Because Christ poured out His own blood to pay the price of sin, we now are forgiven of our many sins. We have help from His Holy Spirit to forgive others. Today examine your heart for any bitterness. Let the blood of Christ cleanse your heart. Pray to forgive your enemies and free yourself from vengeance. God will bring judgment and vengeance in His own time.

*Fearless Love Notes:*

# PERSECUTION
## in South Africa

A few months later I was invited to speak and share my story in South African Churches. It would be a three month speaking tour. I had a wife, a toddler, and an infant who joined me. I had a video of the destruction of my village. I was asked to share the story of the riot and the persecution. One pastor asked if he could make a copy of my video. I thought he meant to make one copy for himself. Instead he made many copies and sent it to Churches all over South Africa. As Christians in South Africa saw the video they were incensed and many Christians demonstrated against the Pakistani Embassy. This demonstration was reported in the paper along with my name and that I was inciting the Christians against Pakistan. Consequently, friends in Pakistan learned that my name was black listed and that the Pakistani police would arrest me as soon as I came home. They warned me not to return to Pakistan for my life was in danger.

*Since 1997 I have not been able to go back to Pakistan and visit my extended family.*

Muslims in South Africa were sent to kill me. God continued to provide a way of escape and thus began a journey for us as we were on the run for two years from July 1997 to July 1999. We would stay in Christian homes for a couple months or a few days. Most places we traveled I ended up speaking and ministering to the local believers.

One day I received a phone call from a Muslim woman whose mother was sick. I was requested to pray for the healing of her mother who was dying from breast cancer. This woman was also the mother of the local Imam (Muslim religious leader) in the area. I told the lady, "Jesus is the healer and Savior and I will pray, fast and ask God to heal your mother." Praise God, in the same week Jesus healed her mother from the breast cancer! The family rejoiced over her healing and began talking about Jesus. But her son who was the Muslim cleric was not happy about her

# Part Two: Chapter 12

praising the name of Jesus. He threatened that he and other Muslims were coming to kill us. It was a very difficult time for my wife and children.

We fled from this area and ended up at a Christian doctor's home. He told me that we were welcome to stay in his home but there was one condition—I must preach in his medical clinic every morning before he sees the patients. I started to preach in his medical clinic. Muslims found out that I was in this town. They appointed people to pursue and kill me. One morning they caught me and wanted me to go to their mosque. They had already told my doctor friend that they wanted to kill me. Praise God, Jesus gave me wisdom and the right words to escape from their grasp. My friend drove me to another city the next day.

We were given a cottage by the Indian Ocean. This was a crowded city, but we felt very alone. We had the pressure of persecution, isolation from close friends and family. We were foreigners and felt the sharp cultural differences from the people around us. We experienced bigotry because of our skin color. We did not have money, a telephone, nor a car. We were dependent on others to provide. I was young, married with two children. Everyday seemed worse and the darkness of depression became a cloud covering my mind. I contemplated taking our family for a walk into the ocean to finish our lives.

At this low point my wife and I decided to pray and fast. We did not sleep in our beds. The next day I was tuning a small short wave radio that had been given to us. I came across Grace To You, by Pastor John MacArthur on FEBA radio. That morning message was meant for me. It washed over me with hope as if God was speaking to me through the radio. That day with tears I was delivered from my suicidal thoughts. I continued to listen to FEBA radio programs during our stay in South Africa. During those difficult days God gave me four pastors to speak into my life and encourage me. I continue to be thankful for these godly pastors and their radio programs; Dr. John MacArthur, and Dr. Charles Swindoll from the United States as well as Pastor Dina Karen and Pastor Ajeet Haroo from India.

## A Vision Of Jesus

Our situation became graver in June 1999. We were informed that our visa would not be renewed and we had fourteen days before our visa would expire. At this point, we were in danger of deportation back to Pakistan where I would face imprisonment or possible death. We had a stamp on our Pakistani Passports that made it illegal for us to travel to any other country without first traveling back to Pakistan. I sought the American Embassy for help. I was rejected. Everywhere we turned seemed to be a dead end. On top of everything else we were out of money and had been asked to leave our present host's home with no place to go. Our only hope was for God to intervene. Even though we were told that we could not get an American visa we decided to apply anyway and trust God for a miracle. My wife was led to fast like Queen Esther of the Bible. (Queen Esther and her servants prayed and did not eat or drink for three days.)

At the end of my wife's three day fast I took the visa application to the American Embassy. I was scared and I prayed that Jesus would escort me to the embassy. As I walked into the embassy I felt like Jesus himself was holding my hand. I went to the window and handed over our Pakistani Passports and visa applications. The embassy clerk did not even look up. She did not ask for a letter of sponsorship from America. To my amazement she took the application and told me to come back in three business days to collect our passports. It was Thursday and I was to come back on Tuesday.

We were amazed and marveled that our visa fees to the United States Embassy had been paid before we had submitted the application. We were told by everyone to obtain this visa would be impossible. A visa of this kind would usually take up to six months and very expensive.

A driver for the Church gave us transportation to and from the Embassy. As I told him of our hope to go to America he asked if I had the money for our plane tickets. I told him "no." Then he asked, "How are you planning to go to America when you need big bucks for plane tickets?" I told him, "I do not have big bucks but I have a big God and He will provide for our plane tickets!"

We had three days before I was to pick up our American visas and one week before our South African visas expired. We did not have any money to pay for the American visas let alone for plane tickets or any other expenses. My wife had just finished a three day complete fast and now I felt led that it is my turn to fast. For three days I did not eat or drink anything but only prayed. I prayed that God would blind the eyes of the embassy officials to the stamp on our passports. I prayed that God would pay for the plane tickets and that He would provide the money for the trip to America. Early Monday morning as my wife and I were praying I saw a vision. Heaven opened and I saw Jesus sitting at the right hand of the Father. I saw a very bright light coming down from Heaven upon my wife and me. The hand of Jesus rose and He said, "it is done!" I did not see the Jesus of popular art work, but He was so glorious that

# Part Two: Chapter 12

I could only look for a glimpse and then put my face on the ground and worship Him. Great joy flooded my soul and I rejoiced as I worshipped the Lord.

The next day after this vision, God provided! Against all odds, we received American visas for our family. This was truly a miracle.

Four days later, a Christian man showed up at our door. He came into the living room and prayed with us. He generously handed us four plane tickets to the United States. He also gave us $416.00 dollars for our expenses. He explained that we were leaving on Thursday, 6pm KLM/Northwest Airlines, six hours short from our expired South African visa, deportation our eventual death. On July 23, 1999 we arrive in the United States, one day before our Pakistani passports' expired. Praise God that He provided at the eleventh hour.

### Ministry In The United States

When we came to the United States we were praying that God would open doors to do His work. We praised God that one day a wonderful brother, David Witt from The Voice of the Martyrs called and wanted to meet us. He introduced us to the amazing ministry of The Voice of the Martyrs. I began to speak for VOM as an Associate Representative.

Since 1997 I have not been able to go back to Pakistan and visit my extended family. (From America, God has helped me build a Bible school in Pakistan and the fourteen original Churches have grown to nearly one hundred Churches.) I now have a national speaking ministry in which I am teaching at seminars and preaching to American Churches on the foundations and the spiritual darkness of Islam. I encourage Christians to the spiritual battle of confronting Muslims with love. Jesus has given me the privilege of seeing many come to Christ and many have received a call to work with Muslims. Christians have been informed on the dangers of Islam and the work in Pakistan has increased. Everywhere around the United States I am asking American Christians to surrender to the spirit of martyrdom. The Holy Spirit has moved on the heart of thousands of Christians to be found faithful to Christ-even unto death.

For all this I thank God for the persecution that my family and I have experienced. I praise God for how He is using Islam as a threat to drive people to Christ and to examine His love as the solution. I was once a Muslim martyr of hate and now by the mercy of Jesus Christ, He has transformed me to become a martyr of love.

**Fearless Love: Meditation**

Mark 10:27, "Looking at them, Jesus said, 'With people it is impossible, but not with God; for all things are possible with God.'" Mujahid was depressed. He was out of time, money and his situation looked impossible. Not only is God big, but he promises to be our Father. The role of a father is to provide and protect. God has a fatherly love for his children and never leaves them or forsakes them. God protected Muhahid miraculously and then provided for his needs and now has given him an international speaking ministry. What are the deepest needs in your life today that look impossible to meet? God is always providing for us but only when those needs have been impossible and beyond our means do we recognize His hand. We have a God of the impossible. God wants you to know His Fatherly love. Pray big prayers today and give him your impossible needs. Big prayers are wonderful opportunities for our big God to show his possible love in our impossible situations.

# Part Two: Chapter 12

## Part 2 Group Discussion And Contemplation

Pray: Ask God to give insight into the deception of a religious spirit, persecution, and the power a transformed life by faith in Jesus Christ.

*Optional Audio Book: Play Disc 2, Track 1,*
*Attack By Muslim Mobs—for five minutes*

Imagine that you were a Pakistani Christian living in Pakistan. What are some of the ways your life would be different from the life you live today? Economically? Politically? Socially? Spiritually?

Tens of thousands of Muslims rioted against the Christians of Shanti Niger because they thought the Christians tore a Qur'an and threw it to the ground. What issues in your community would cause the whole community to march together in passionate protest? Is the passion of the Muslims that rioted against the Christians of Shanti Niger inspiring or abhorrent to you? Explain your answer. When is passion appropriate?

There is great religious confusion in Pakistan today. The Islamic world is full of many sects that fight against one another. In what way do you see religious confusion within the Christian world? In what ways do you see God bringing hope and unity?

Have you witnessed the fruit of the Spirit from the people or ministries in your life? (love, joy, peace, patience, kindness, goodness, faithfulness, gentleness, and self-control.)

When Mujahid converted to be a Muslim he began to live a double life. Many Christians in Islamic nations have found themselves in the same situation. Is this wrong that Christians have double lives to escape persecution and discrimination? What would you do?

In the beginning of chapter 9 Mujahid quotes 2 Timothy 2:13: "...if we are faithless, he will remain faithful, for he cannot disown himself." Can you think of some commitments to God or ways in which you have been faithless? In what ways did you find God's grace and faithfulness in these situations?

A verse that changed Mujahid's life forever was John 14:6: "Jesus said, 'I am the way, the truth, and the life, and no one shall come to the Father except through me.'" Is there any other way for Muslims to receive salvation other than faith in Jesus Christ according to Jesus Himself? Do you agree with the following statement? "The greatest kindness that you can give to a Muslim or anyone looking for peace is faith in Jesus Christ." Explain your answer.

Soon after Mujahid's conversion he was called to be a pastor. He did not like this calling because of the personal sacrifice that it involved. Ephesians 2:10 says, "For we are His workmanship, created in Christ Jesus for good works, which God prepared beforehand so that we would walk in them." All children of God have a calling and purpose that God prepared from the foundations of the earth. What good works does God call you to do? How does it involve personal sacrifice? In what ways have you found your calling rewarding?

During Mujahid's early ministry he was able to start 14 churches. He gives credit to the Holy Spirit working salvation and miracles in his life to found these churches. How is your local church growing today? In regards to growth would the Holy Spirit or man's leadership receive more credit? Why or why not? How can you make a difference in your church regarding this situation?

## Part Two: Chapter 12

Tens of thousands of Muslims rioted and burned the possessions of the Christians because they thought the Christians tore a Qur'an. Reflect on chapter one regarding jihad. In what ways did the Islamic principle of jihad contribute to this riot?

What would be harder? To lose all your possessions in a violent riot or forgive the ones who rioted against you? Why is forgiveness so hard? Why are possessions so hard to loss? What made a more powerful statement, the rioting of the Muslims for the Qur'an or the Christians forgiving their enemies? Why?

Mujahid prayed for a Muslim lady with breast cancer and God healed her. Her son was a Muslim cleric that was angry when she praised Jesus for her healing. Why is praising the name of Jesus so threatening to this Islamic leader? Have you seen ways that God has blessed people and they would not praise the name of Jesus?

Mujahid's testimony is a powerful contrast of a life that was given to Islamic martyrdom and now his life is transformed to be a witness of the love of Christ. Does his life give you hope for the Islamic world? Why or why not?

**Witness:** Do an internet search of Christians living in Pakistan or other Islamic nations. Read an article about some of the events and issues they have to deal with. Share Mujahid's story with some co-workers or schoolmates this week. Ask God to grant the blessing of running into one Muslim this week. Make it your goal to smile at them and say hello and then shoot a prayer of intercession on their behalf that God open the eyes of their heart to the light of the love of Jesus Christ.

**Personal Application:** Ask God to reveal the areas of your life that you have a religious prideful spirit. Practice praying and loving those outside your religious camp with actions of love. Think about how Jesus would reach out to them. Look for scriptures this week that talk about loving your enemies. How can you apply those scriptures to the enemies in your life?

**Digging Deeper:** To hear and view more testimonies of Muslims transformed by the grace of Jesus Christ go to www.MuslimEducationCenter.com/testimonies

**Ending Prayer:** Pray through the points and insights that you gained.

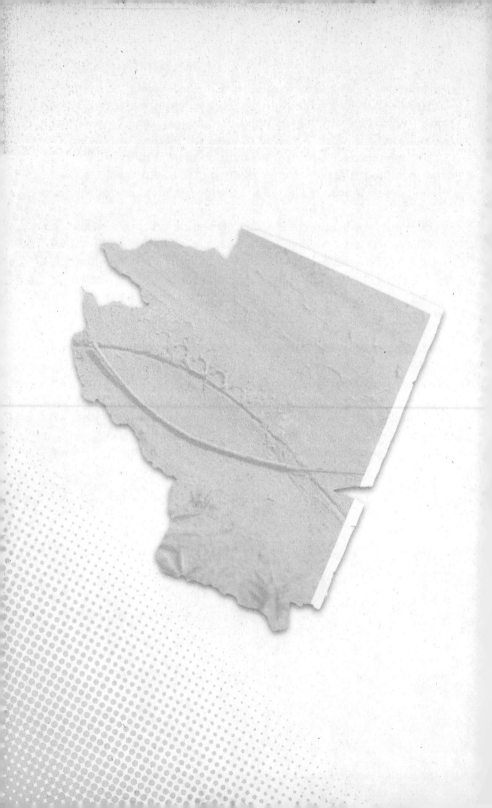

## Part Three:
# LIVING
### *Martyrs*

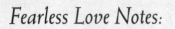

*Fearless Love Notes:*

# THE ADVANCING
## *Persecuted Church*

M artyrdom is the ultimate act of love to all the disciples of Jesus Christ! The call of Biblical martyrdom is the antithesis of the call of Islamic martyrdom. The motivation of Biblical martyrdom is love. "Greater love has no one than this, that one lay down his life for his friends." (John 15:13) Jesus was called a friend of sinners. "All have sinned and fallen short of the Glory of God." (Romans 3:23) For the Christian this means that we must lay our lives down for all people.

In a nutshell, Islamic martyrdom is accomplished by the violent destruction of the enemies of Islam. Biblical martyrdom is the sacrifice and death of the disciples of Christ for the benefit of their enemies. Persecution of Christians is simply God's love demonstrated in sacrificial suffering by living or dying as a martyr.

### Persecution of Christians

Christians account for 2 billion of the 6 billion people in the world. Christians as a whole are the largest discriminated and persecuted minority group in the world. Today more than half of the earth's population lives in restricted nations where they risk persecution for becoming believers in Jesus Christ. The Voice of the Martyrs (VOM) is a non-profit, interdenominational organization with a vision for aiding Christians around the world who are being persecuted for their faith in Christ, fulfilling the Great Commission, and educating the world about the ongoing persecution of Christians.

VOM defines restricted nations as, "countries where government policy or practice prevent Christians from obtaining Bibles or other Christian literature. Also included are government-sanctioned circumstances where Christians are harassed, imprisoned, killed or deprived of their possessions or liberties because of their faith in Jesus."[i]

Fifty-one nations are named as restricted or hostile regarding religious freedom for Christians. These Christians are limited legally and socially in their expression of faith. Of these fifty-one nations thirty-three are considered Islamic nations with Muslims being in the majority.[ii] Islamic nations have become the number one persecutors of Christians. Yet, under constant hostility, the gospel is thriving and exploding in some of these countries.

Richard and Sabina Wurmbrand founded The Voice of the Martyrs in 1967. This Romanian Jewish couple were professing atheists. In their late twenties they discovered their Messiah, Jesus Christ. Richard became a pastor and a major Christian leader within his country. He was

> Truth changes us; we do not change the Truth. Truth at times will cause us suffering and pain. These words mean more as we consider that Jesus is the Truth

tortured and endured a total of fourteen years imprisonment for his faith under the Communist rule. His book, Tortured for Christ, is a Christian classic and has been translated in over 65 different languages and millions of copies have been distributed around the world. In October 2006, Romanian Television surveyed the Romanian citizens and elected Richard Wurmbrand the fifth most influential figure in the history of Romania. During his imprisonment, Sabina was a faithful partner to Richard continuing their Church work. She spent three years in forced labor camps because her faith. She told me once, "Martyrs do not make Truth, but Truth makes martyrs."

Truth changes us; we do not change the Truth. Truth at times will cause us suffering and pain. These words mean more as we consider that Jesus is the Truth. Therefore, Truth is not a concept, but is in the person of Jesus Christ. Scripture promised that all followers of Him will suffer. (2 Timothy 3:12)

Many seasons of history record the Truth of Christ growing and spreading under persecution. Like a wildflower seed in the desert, the gospel thrives through the winds and storms of difficulty in hostile environments. The wind of trial is an instrument of God's grace for the growth of the gospel, and the storm's rain helps the roots grow and deepen. For those who have the eyes to see, persecution is a tool of God in maturing his Church and directing his disciples. The United States of America was founded by believers in Jesus fleeing religious persecution of Europe. Today, Christians are still fleeing persecution and seeking refuge in America. I meet them all the time. Many of them are from

Islamic nations. They have a story to tell us if we will listen.

Jesus promised, "If they persecuted Me, they will also persecute you." (John 15:20) Today seeds of the gospel are being spread. Some Christians will be put to death. Some will be beaten, and others will remain in prison. In many places Christians are meeting in secret. It is dangerous for them to bring their Bible (if they even have one). Yet they have found the risk to be a reasonable sacrifice. I hope that you might gain understanding of their suffering love, and in the end, fellowship in their suffering and sacrifice. (Philippians 3:10) God designed each of us to be living martyrs- faithful unto death.

A transformed life in Jesus Christ is a life of motion in faith and action. The Bible says, "All men will hate you because of me, but he who stands firm to the end will be saved. When you are persecuted in one place, flee to another. I tell you the truth, you will not finish going through the cities of Israel before the Son of Man comes." (Matthew 10:22-23 NIV) Christian refugees fleeing from one place to another is the normal life for many persecuted believers. During my trip to Sudan, Africa I was told that there were over three million displaced Sudanese, most of them are Christians. The Apostle Peter referred to Christians as "strangers" in this world. (1 Peter 2:11) Christian believers in persecuted areas understand feelings of being a stranger. Jesus tells us that He is the great shepherd of the sheep. He states in the great commission, "Go and make disciples…" (Matthew 28:19). Sheep may resist going to other pastures. Like sheep dogs nipping at the heels of the sheep, persecution nips at the heels of believers driving them forward. Persecution drives the people of God forward in the spread of the gospel.

### Witnesses Of Christ

Richard Wurmbrand intently listened to a report from VOM workers who had just returned from Sudan. The team had been distributing aid to Christian refugees when they were attacked by the Sudanese Islamic troops. They witnessed the death of Sudanese Christians and the burning of villages. They barely escaped with their lives. Once they finished telling their story, Pastor Wurmbrand thoughtfully commented, "No longer are you a missionary. You are now a witness." These are profound words. The word missionary does not exist in the Bible! The word "witness" is used. We are to witness or testify to what God has done in our lives and the lives of others around the world.

Let us reflect upon those words: "No longer a missionary, but a witness." The calling is simply to be a witness of Christ's love, grace and His glory that abides in us. The old hymn, Amazing Grace expresses it well: "Once I was lost, but now I am found...blind, but now I see." We invite the lost to the glory of God's Truth. Whether they accept our message is not our problem, God only calls us to be a witness of the Truth." God is calling us past the "missionary" endeavor to convert Muslims to Christianity. We are simply to be His witnesses of the love of Christ to Muslims.

> **"No longer are you a missionary. You are now a witness."**

In Muslim nations around the world, Christians are persecuted, because they are witnessing agents of God. Christians in persecuted areas cannot stay in their comfort zone. Their faith is being tested and their lives are being put on display for non-believers and believers to observe. Jesus said, "And I, if I am lifted up from the earth, I will draw all to Myself." (John 12:32 ALT) Christ was referring to the suffering he was to endure on the cross as well as his resurrection. He knew that the display of his passion and persecution would be the vehicle of redemption. Likewise, when Christians are lifted up on their own crosses of persecution and suffering, the life of Christ is again displayed for the world to see, and all people are drawn unto Christ.

### The Gospel Is Growing Where There Are Martyrs

Jesus declared his paradigm of proclamation in Acts 1:8: "But you shall receive power when the Holy Spirit has come upon you; and you shall be My witnesses both in Jerusalem, and in all Judea and Samaria, and even to the remotest part of the earth." Again here is the key Biblical word, witnesses. This word is translated from the Greek word martus. We get our English word martyr from martus. This word martus incorporates the legal witness, observation, and personal conviction to suffer and lose ones life in the proclamation of faith. In the most literal sense Jesus declares that His children will receive His spirit of martyrdom. Christ's spirit will be a witnessing force to bring the gospel to the ends of the earth. In the simplest form I like to define martus as sharing your faith at great cost or sacrifice. The ultimate sacrifice is of course the loss of one's life. The daily loving sacrifice of believers is living in Christ's spirit of martyrdom.

When we understand this perspective we can begin to understand what God is doing and why there is such hope for the world today.

Around the world where people say "there is no hope," there is hope, because the world is full of martyrs of love willing to lay their lives down for grace and Truth.

An Iranian believer told me, once a Muslim becomes a believer in Jesus, he will not live longer than a few years. Iran is not an easy country in which to worship Christ. In 2008 the Iranian leadership passed a law of death sentence to all who convert to Christianity or influence other Muslims to convert. A few years ago I traveled to Iran and met a Muslim background believer. He is secretly involved in the underground Church, and sharing the gospel. Because of his faith in Jesus, he has been arrested and beaten three times. Five times his family was forcibly evicted and made homeless. Yet his family continues to live by faith and build up other secret believers in their country. A few months before my visit, VOM gave him a car for his ministry. As I met him outside the hotel I greeted him with, "Hallelujah!" (Which means praise the Lord!) "Hallelujah," is the universal language of love between believers. His face lit up as he said "Hallelujah." We embraced, experiencing the love all believers have for one another. With great excitement he began telling me how he has put that word on the back of his car. His English was broken and this just didn't sound right. To have "Hallelujah" plastered on the back of your car in Iran sounded pretty dangerous to me. Sure enough when we went out to the car, I looked at the back window and there it was—"Hallelujah." He wasn't kidding. He had been beaten three times, but the blows have moved him toward Jesus, not away. I saw fearlessness about him. His joy flowed as we talked. He shared with me that there is an underground Church in every major city in Iran. Lives are being transformed and the gospel is shared in Iran because of fearless living martyrs like this brother in Christ.

# Part Three: Chapter 13

### Fearless Love: Meditation

Every life is a testimony to someone. To what does your life testify? It has been said, "A life is soon to pass, only what is done in Christ will last." You will leave a witness to Christ or to someone or something else. When we become children of God, He gives us His spirit of love. Romans 5:5 says, "because the love of God has been poured out within our hearts through the Holy Spirit who was given to us." It is Christ's Holy Spirit that testifies to love. His spirit of love can also be called a spirit of martyrdom. Christ's spirit in His children cannot be hidden. Love by design reaches out and witnesses its desire to the lost, hurting and broken world. If you know Christ today then you know love and the world will bear witness to the love enwrapped in you.

### Fearless Love: Endnotes

i    *The Voice of the Martyrs, Special Issue 2008, www.persecution.com*

ii   *The Voice of the Martyrs, Special Issue 2008, www.persecution.com*

*Fearless Love Notes:*

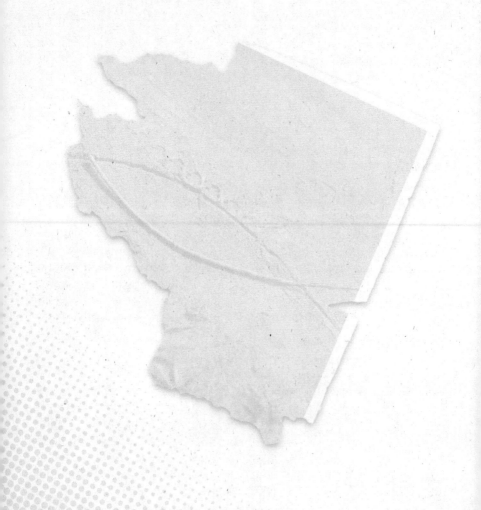

# SUFFERING
*For His Glory*

Philippians 1:29 says, "For it has been granted on behalf of Christ, not only to believe in Him, but to suffer for Him." Part of God's plan for his disciples is to suffer. I know when these words are spoken in America they sound horrific, but this statement is Biblical. Jesus promised suffering. "In this world you will have trouble." Jesus ended

> "Real gold fears no fire." The fire is the vessel that brings the purity.

that verse by saying "Be of good cheer, for I have overcome the world." (John 16:33) The glory of God is revealed when there is purpose in pain. Purposeless pain brings despair and depression, but purposeful pain brings glory and hope. We are not called to suffer for suffering sake, but for glory!

I have heard Chinese believers describe sanctification (spiritual maturity) as suffering for Jesus. When I was in China I certainly saw many expressions of suffering for His glory. One day my friend Montie and I visited an underground Bible school being held in a typical Chinese apartment. The house Church pastors had discreetly slipped into this apartment where they would live for 20 days, morning, noon, and night. It is too dangerous for all these believers to go in and out of the apartment for fear of drawing attention. One morning I discreetly met with these believers. Walking through the doorway, I observed a four inch thick pad of foam attached to the door in order to absorb the sound. This group of believers starts every day by whispering hymns and songs of praise. I felt the Lord speaking to my heart saying, "David, when you want to be intimate with me, be like the Chinese. Crawl up in my lap, whisper into my ear, because your worship is not intended for anyone else." It is a beautiful picture of experiencing intimacy with God. Some of the most beautiful acts of love are done in quiet.

We were privileged to hear the testimony of the Chinese house Church pastor in this apartment training center. This particular pastor oversaw fifty-thousand believers. I would never have guessed the significance of his leadership by his gentleness and humble spirit. He had earned his stripes. Five times, he told us, he was arrested and beaten.

# Part Three: Chapter 14

Three times they gave him electric shock torture to elicit the names of believers and locations of house Churches. He refused to be counted as a Judas, and he remained faithful by not revealing any information about the unregistered Churches. Chinese Christians understand that every name or place mentioned leads to more arrests and beatings. They are determined to keep this information to themselves, even if they have to suffer for it. Proverbs 25:2 says that it is to the glory of God to conceal a matter. This pastor counted his torture as light affliction compared to the glory of God that He had experienced.

Because living martyrs like this Chinese brother are witnessing the gospel, China is currently exploding with new converts. The Chinese Church is estimated to be over a 100 million believers strong and growing daily. Secret Bible schools scattered throughout China are training Chinese believers to bring the gospel to the Muslim people of China and throughout Asia. What many people do not know is that there are an estimated 29 million Muslims in China alone.

## Back to Jerusalem Movement

The Chinese House Church leaders are calling this new momentum of evangelism The Back to Jerusalem Movement. They are praying that one-hundred thousand Chinese will be trained and sent out from China towards the city of Jerusalem. These evangelists will proclaim the gospel of Jesus Christ to the Muslims, Hindus and Buddhists they meet along the way. This is a very significant number considering that full time missionaries sent out from United States of America presently number around forty-five thousand. Chinese leaders believe many will die in the process of planting the Word of Christ across Asia. Chinese believers confess that they are willing to die for the honor of sharing His love.

Why would these Chinese Christians be willing to risk their lives to love Muslims by sharing the gospel of Jesus Christ? I believe they have a spirit of martyrdom. They understand the value of testifying about God's grace in their own lives, and in loving others into the kingdom of God, one person at a time. "But you will receive power when the Holy Spirit comes on you, and you will be my witnesses." (Acts 1:8) God's plan is being revealed. He is bringing His glory to the world and He is doing it through the martyrs. The wisdom of the worldly wise is confounded. Randy Alcorn in his book, *Safely Home* quotes a Chinese believer who says, "Real gold fears no fire." The fire is the vessel that brings the purity.

**Transformation in Turkey**

During a trip to Turkey I met a Turkish pastor who shared that in 1972 he knew of only ten Turkish believers in Jesus. He told me that for nine-hundred years there was no historical evidence of a Turkish Church. During that time Christianity was present in Turkey only in minority ethnic groups. The pastor said, "They showed us Christianity, but they never showed us Christ." When Christianity is only a culture, the penetrating power to bring light into spiritual darkness is weak. When comfort and tradition are more valued than proclamation and regeneration, Christianity is operating only as another religion. Christ is revealed by love. And love is revealed by sacrifice.

Todd Nettleton, VOM coworker, and I met another Turkish believer who had been arrested the year before. He distributed gospel tracts and Bibles on the street. For his gospel work he spent 30 days in prison. The first night of imprisonment he felt afraid and alone. He prayed and wept asking God to free him. Then Lord spoke to his heart and said, "Didn't you pray and ask me to use you?" At that moment his self pity broke, and he realized his doubt in God's faithfulness. He repented and praised God. He recalled it as the sweetest night of joyous loving communion he ever had. Every day in prison for the next thirty days, he preached the gospel for three hours to Muslim prisoners.

When we asked, "Are you still distributing gospel tracts and Bibles?" He answered, "Every day, brother!"

Why? It's going to cost him! He is a living martyr. He has discovered joy in suffering for Christ. He receives pleasure seeing the lives of the lost Islamic souls changed by God's forgiveness. "Blessed are those who are persecuted."(Matthew 5:10)

# Part Three: Chapter 14

### Fearless Love: Mediation

Michaelangelo was asked while carving the famed King David statue how he knew what parts of the stone to chisel. He replied. "It is easy, I simply chip away the parts that are not David" Christ sees His perfect image in us and He chisels away all that does not reflect His image. A quote at the beginning of the chapter says, "purposeful pain brings glory and hope." God uses persecution and trial to bring forth His perfect image. 1 John 3:2, "Beloved, now we are children of God, and it has not appeared as yet what we will be. We know that when He appears, we will be like Him..." Perfect love is Christ likeness! Your pain is the chisel chipping off what is not like Christ. You can have hope because His work in your life is perfecting His love and bringing forth future glory. Thank the Lord that He is making you beautiful and that you can trust His hand on the chisel throughout your life. Pray for all Christian around the world facing suffering and persecution that they might find joy by the assurance of their future glory.

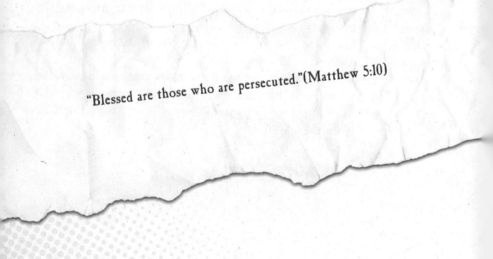

"Blessed are those who are persecuted."(Matthew 5:10)

*Fearless Love Notes:*

*Fearless Love Notes:*

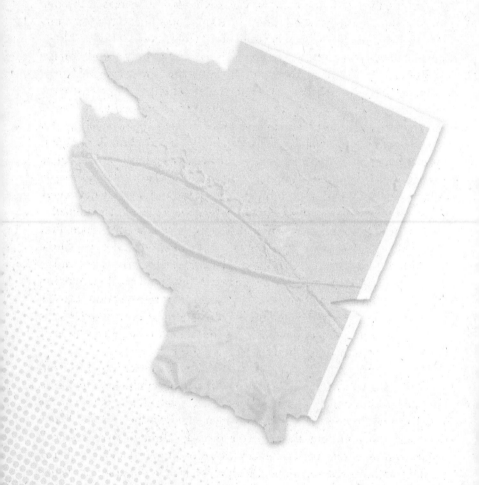

# WHAT IS LACKING
## In Christ's Afflictions

The world tangibly experiences the sacrificial love of Christ through the lives of living martyrs. God's Kingdom is increased through persecution. Matthew 11:12 (NIV): "the kingdom of heaven is forcefully advancing, and forceful men lay hold of it." Colossians 1:24 says: "Now I rejoice in what was suffered for you." This verse certainly sounds foreign to our ears. Is Saint Paul, the writer of Colossians, a masochist? There is something very mysterious about rejoicing in suffering. According to the world's mindset it sounds absolutely foolish. Paul goes on to say "and I fill up in my flesh what is still lacking in regards to Christ's afflictions, for the sake of his body, which is the Church." What is Paul speaking about? What is lacking in the afflictions of Christ? Was Paul somehow fulfilling something Jesus didn't complete on the cross? Paul's writings clarify that when Jesus said "it is finished," the penalty of sin was destroyed. Justification and atonement through Christ were completely fulfilled.

I heard Dr. John Piper comment on this verse at a conference. Paul declares that Christ suffers through his (Paul's) body. Likewise Christ still suffers through His Church (His disciples). Christ is now at the right hand of the Father, so the one thing he will not do is to return in His physical body and suffer again for His creation. He will not be crucified all over again. The next time he comes, he returns as a ruling king. Therefore, Christ suffers vicariously through his Church which is all of His disciples.

Christ said to Saul, (whose name was later changed to Paul) "Saul, Saul, why do you persecute me!" It is important to note that Jesus did not say 'his children', but 'me.' Jesus said that the way you treat the least of my children is the way you treat me. (Matthew 25:40) When you suffer in your flesh, through your diseases, through your economic trials, through your marital difficulties, through your family problems, and through your persecutions, Christ is revealed in the suffering. When the world sees the fruit of love, joy, peace, patience, kindness, goodness, faithfulness, gentleness, and self-control, (Galatians 5:22-23) in the midst of these difficulties, then they say, "Surely, there must be a God."

This allows us to say with Paul that we now rejoice in our sufferings because we are participating in the suffering of the Body of Christ for God's divine purposes. We partake in the suffering of persecuted believers worldwide. It's not random. Their suffering isn't necessarily because they made a bad decision today. It is because God has a purpose through it. Our suffering has a purpose. 2 Corinthians 4:11 says: "for we who are alive are always being given over to death for Jesus' sake, so that his life may be revealed in our mortal body."

### Beaten With A Stick For Jesus—Mujahid's Story.

Immediately when I became a believer in Jesus the Holy Spirit filled me with such a great joy and zeal in my heart that I began sharing the gospel with everyone. I did not know much theology or how to preach the Gospel. All I knew was that Jesus is the Son of God and that he had died for my sins on the cross. I was like a beggar in the streets. Everyone I ran into I would beg them to give me a minute of their time and then I shared the love and forgiveness of sins through Christ. About a week after I received Christ, I met a Muslim friend with whom I had gone to school. I explained to him about the hope and life I had found in Christ. He repented of his sins and asked Christ into his life as we prayed together. Upon arriving home that evening he shared his new faith in Jesus with his family.

His father sent word to me to come to their home because he wanted to talk to me about what I shared with his son. They live out in the country, with sheep, goats, oxen, and cows. They own a big home with many rooms. I walked to their home with much joy because I thought they also wanted to receive Christ. The father answered the door and invited me to their back room. He and I went into the back room and he locked the door behind me. He mockingly said to me, "Now call on your God, I am going to beat you. He took a stick three feet long by three inches thick which Pakistanis use for leading oxen. He began to beat me on my back, legs and rear. He screamed at me, "I am more powerful than your God. Where is your God now?" As he beat me, I didn't fight back but I cried from the sting of the cane. This was my first experience in being beaten for the name of Jesus. In my mind I thought of Jesus on the cross crying out in pain and asking the Father to forgive His enemies. After a few minutes of beating, the rest of his family heard the commotion and began banging on the door for their father to stop. He stopped the beating, opened the door and told me to leave. I told him, "I do not hold this against you and I forgive you." Considering that I had only recently been a man full of hate, this was quite a miracle for me.

## Be Faithful Unto Death

"We live in days that are precarious. A few years ago, a coworker of mine, visited Pakistan. During a Christian worship service, he saw the believers put their left hand to their throat and lift the right hand in the air. He was told by the Pastor they were demonstrating Revelation 2:10 "Be faithful until death, and I will give you the crown of life." They put their hand to their throat to represent their death and lifted the other hand up in surrender to God. These Pakistani believers were demonstrating a spirit of martyrdom. They desired to be faithful to Christ and His love unto death. They are living martyrs. They stand strong as a minority in an Islamic land full of violence, fear and threats.

### Forgive Your Enemies

Zeba is a beautiful Christian girl in Pakistan. At the age of ten she was a housekeeper for a Muslim family. Her Muslim employer noticed her beauty and decided she would be a good wife to their son. They demanded Zeba become a Muslim. "No, I can't become a Muslim, because I am a Christian" replied Zeba. Although she did not know how to read, she remained faithful to Christ and was beaten three times for refusing to learn verses from the Qur'an. She ran home after the third beating. They then accused her of stealing. It was a Muslim's word against a Christian's word. Her mom defended Zeba before her accuser. She asked, "How can you accuse my Zeba of stealing? She is a good worker! She is a Christian. You know she has never stolen anything. Please, drop the charges," she pleaded. With rising anger the Muslim man replied, "You accuse me of lying?" He began to beat Zeba's mom until she was unconscious. Then he grabbed a can of gasoline, doused her body and lit her on fire; Zeba's mom died. This man was never charged with murder.

When I visited Zeba, I saw great pain and grief from the loss of her Mother. I asked Zeba if she was able to forgive the Muslim man who murdered her mom. Slowly and with difficulty she replied, "No." Our

> They are living martyrs. They stand strong as a minority in an Islamic land full of violence, fear and threats.

team talked about the power of forgiveness that Christ gave us through His Spirit. Miraculously, Zeba prayed with us to forgive the Muslim man who had murdered her Mom.

How can she offer forgiveness with such injustice? This man has not asked for forgiveness, but Zeba has the supernatural Spirit of Christ living in her. She is a living martyr.

The Bible says "Those who sow in tears shall reap in joyful shouting." (Psalms 126:5) I saw expressions of great joy on the face of Zeba as God brought waves of healing to her heart. She shared with us that she wants to become a Bible school teacher. Today one of my favorite pictures is Zeba with a huge smile on her face, sitting next to her sewing machine. She has a new hope and faith in the provision of God.

God gives us direction on how to be free from sin in 1 Peter 4:1. "Therefore as Christ suffered, let us arm ourselves with the same attitude, for those who have suffered in the flesh are done away with sin." Many Christians in the West are addicted to one sin or another. The Bible gives the clear path of freedom from sin - suffering for righteousness sake.

### Living Martyrs

God has ordained every one of his children to be a living, witnessing martyr. The day the power of the Holy Spirit comes upon us, we become living martyrs. In our lives we too will have seasons of suffering. Be not afraid. These times will be our opportunity to proclaim the Truth and walk free from sin. The presence of Christ through these trials make the suffering moments feel small, yet victorious. I have heard persecuted believers say that suffering for Jesus is not really suffering because He brings us so much peace and joy!

This is what the Scripture has to say in Hebrews 13:5(NIV), " 'Never will I leave you; never will I forsake you.' So we say with confidence, 'The Lord is my helper; I will not be afraid. What can man do to me?'" They can beat me, they can slander me, they can persecute me, and through it all I am blessed, because the Lord is my helper. Jesus said "... do not be afraid of those who kill the body but cannot kill the soul. Rather, be afraid of the One who can destroy both soul and body in hell." (Matthew 10:28)

Islamic terrorists are being conquered by the love of living Christian martyrs. Often when Muslims comes to Christ it costs them everything. They are rejected by their families. They lose their jobs. They lose their friends. They find poverty, rejection and insults as their companions. Death threats are a living reality. Living martyrdom is the call of every

Muslim background believer in Jesus Christ. No student is greater than his teacher. Comfortable Christians will produce more comfortable Christians. Martyrs will produce more martyrs.

A common phrase among persecuted believers is, "where there is a cross there is a crown, no cross, no crown." In the Islamic world, the jewels lining the crowns of the martyrs will be the Muslim lives won to Christ due to their love, sacrifice and suffering.

Gods calls all of us to be living martyrs. God uses our lives as a living witness. In part four we will examine how God uses our death as a witness for Him. God has ordained that we not only live as martyrs but we will die as martyrs (witnesses). Read on for the great hope which comes when greater purpose is found in dying for what you know is Truth.

### Fearless Love: Meditation

If you have faith in Christ you can directly relate your faith to others who took risks, sacrificed and showed kindness to you. God reveals Himself through creation and His children. The human experience interprets God's love or lack of love from their personal experiences in this fallen, broken and wicked world. In fact, all of our understanding of God and resulting faith is due to our experiences. 1 John 4:19, " We love, because He first loved us." The love of God was demonstrated with Jesus coming in flesh to love us first, that we might love Him, and then others. No one can go to God because He is Holy and separated in His perfect heaven. So God came to us as a man. His Holy Spirit now lives in every one of His children that have accepted by faith the gift of His life. He laughs when they laugh and He hurts when they hurt. What have your experienced in this life regarding the nature of God? If you do not know the love of God, pray that God will lead your footsteps to a real Christian. Watch their life. You will experience Christ. The light of Christ abides in all His children even if it might be dim at times. If Christ is alive in your life today pray that you might be his vessel of love to others through risk, sacrifice and kindness that demonstrates His grace not only to the Muslim world but to anyone you meet.

# Part Three: Chapter 15

## Part 3 Group Discussion And Contemplation

Pray: Ask God to give insight into the spirit of the living martyrs.

*Optional Audio Book: Play Disc 2, Track 15-16,*
*Forgive Your Enemies—for six minutes*

In Chapter 13 the statistic is mentioned: "Christians as a whole are the largest discriminated and persecuted minority group in the world." Before reading this book had you ever thought about the current world wide persecution of Christians? Why do you think the persecution of Christians is so large today and so few people are aware of the problem? Why do you think the government, media and leaders do not focus more on this issue?

"We do not change Truth, Truth changes us." What do you think this statement means? How do you understand Truth? Has Truth changed you? If so, in what ways?

Are you a witness for Christ? Why or Why not?

How would you describe sanctification (spiritual maturity) in your own life? How have the things you have suffered in your life affected you? Are you a better or worse person today because of what you have suffered? Explain.

Chinese believers have stated that they are willing to give their lives in the witness of Jesus Christ to Muslims. Is this a statement of foolishness or inspiration to you? Why?

The pastor in Turkey is quoted with, "They showed us Christianity, but they never showed us Christ." What do you think that statement means? Could you say the same statement is true in your own area? How do you know the difference between cultural Christianity and Biblical Christianity?

When persecuted believers suffer around the world does Christ feel their pain? How does Christ suffer with His Church today? Matthew 25:37-40,(ESV) "Then the righteous will answer him, saying, 'Lord, when did we see you hungry and feed you, or thirsty and give you drink? And when did we see you a stranger and welcome you, or naked and clothe you? And when did we see you sick or in prison and visit you?' And the King will answer them, 'Truly, I say to you, as you did it to one of the least of these my brothers, you did it to me.'"

When you suffer does Christ suffer? Why or why not? 1 Corinthians 12:26, "And if one member suffers, all the members suffer with it; if one member is honored, all the members rejoice with it." How do all members of Christ's Body share in each other's suffering and rejoicing?

Zeba's mom was martyred. Zeba forgave the murderer even when he did not ask. Should she have forgiven the man even though the man was not asking for forgiveness? Why is forgiveness so powerful? When is forgiveness not appropriate? Can human beings truly forgive without divine intervention? Why or Why not?

## Part Three: Chapter 15

The murderer of Zeba's mom was never charged with a crime. What is the difference between forgiveness and justice? Can you have forgiveness and justice at the same time? Will this man ever receive justice? How?

What does the phrase, "Comfortable Christians will produce more comfortable Christians. Martyrs will produce more martyrs," mean to you? As a Christian is it good to produce more martyrs? After reading this section do you consider yourself a living martyr? Why or why not?

How will the identity of being a living martyr increase or decrease a personal witness of Jesus Christ?

**Witness:** Look for stories this week in the media that deal with persecution, discrimination and human rights abuses. Think about the world views(religious views) that motivate this kind of injustice. Are Christians mentioned or hinted as being involved? Pray for the persecutors and the victims of these stories. Pray for the persecuted Christian minority in Islamic nations. Pray that the Lord would bless you this week by meeting a Muslim and enjoying a pleasant conversation with them.

**Personal Application:** Think about what it means to be a living martyr in your life. How can you begin to live more courageous this week? Make a list of fears and ask God to give you His martus spirit in overcoming them. Make a goal to overcome one fear with an action of faith this week.

**Digging Deeper:** To hear more stories of God's purposes of living martyrs overcoming suffering and persecution: Go to www.SpiritofMartyrdom.com and then link to "Multimedia" hear more talks and stories from David Witt.

**Ending Prayer:** Pray through the points and insights that you gained.

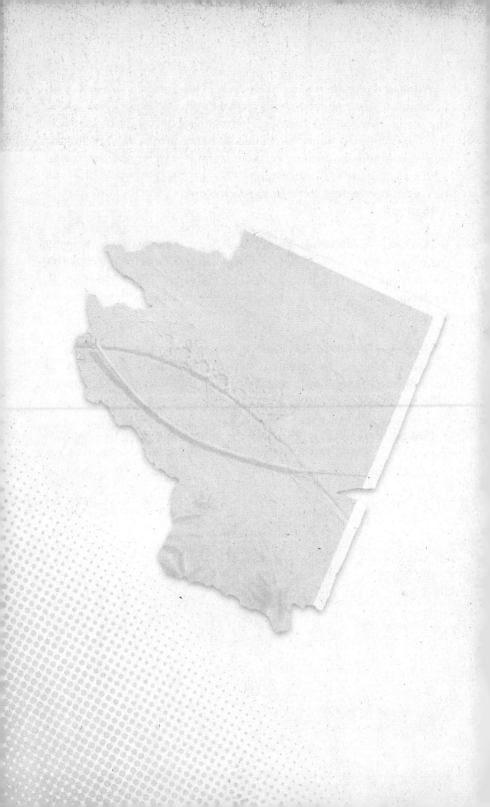

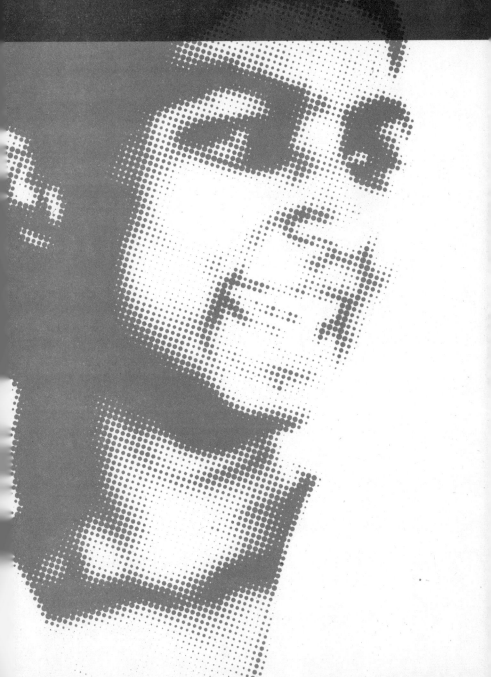

*Part Four:*
# DYING TO SHARE JESUS

*Fearless Love Notes:*

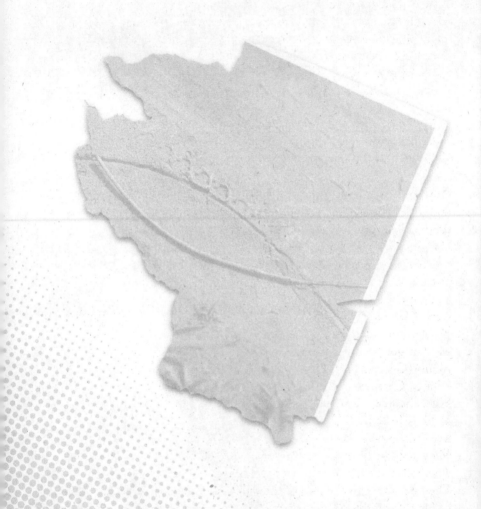

# BLOOD OF THE MARTYRS
*In Pakistan*

One Sunday morning in a Pakistani village, five Muslim men, armed with automatic rifles entered a Church where the congregation was still assembled. They were celebrating God's provision through the many difficulties they had been facing. Pastor Emanuel was preaching on remaining faithful to Christ. One of the gunmen walked up the center aisle and confronted Pastor Emanuel. At gunpoint, the Muslim man demanded that the pastor throw down his Bible. Allowing a Bible to touch the carpet or the ground in Pakistan is considered sacrilegious. Pastor Emanuel would not be intimidated. For twenty years he had faithfully shepherded the flock of Jesus Christ. He told the gunman he would not throw down his Bible. He held the Bible to his chest and turned his body to shield the Scriptures. At that moment, the first shots rang out. Pastor Emanuel was killed instantly. Then, the gunmen turned their rifles on the congregation. As they were shooting the Christians they called out "Allah Akbar," which translates, "Allah is Greater". Then they cried out, "graveyard to Christians in Pakistan and Afghanistan, this is just the start." Hundreds of bullets rang out and ultimately nineteen Christians were martyred.

Isn't it interesting that the Muslim gunmen were worshipping Allah (God of the Qur'an) while killing Christians. Little did they know that they were fulfilling the words of Jesus in John 16:1-4a (NIV): "All this I have told you so that you will not go astray. They will put you out of the synagogue; in fact, a time is coming when anyone who kills you will think he is offering a service to God. They do such things because they have not known the Father or me. I have told you this, so that when the time comes you will remember that I warned you."

*The world cannot understand how the gospel can grow in such a violent environment.*

Some Christians in the village wanted to seek revenge and burn the Mosques and kill the Muslims. However, the pastors calmed their rage by reminding these believers of the power of forgiveness through Jesus

Christ. They told them that this tragedy is a struggle against sin. The Muslim men were deceived in their sin like Saul in the book of Acts who in his ignorance persecuted and approved the killing of the disciple Stephen. The Church leaders explained that the appropriate response is to forgive and love our enemies. Charity and forgiveness broke out toward the Muslims in the Christian community.

One of the Muslim teachers addressed the crowd at the memorial service. He said he was ashamed of the behavior of some of the Muslims in his country. He declared that the Christians had shown that they were true Pakistanis through their loving conduct and their forgiveness toward those Muslims. "Christians as 'true Pakistanis, in the Islamic Republic of Pakistan?' We have never heard those words before," said one of the witnesses. Maybe the blood of the martyrs had sprinkled on the heart of this Islamic teacher and it has begun to crack open his soul. Certainly all the Muslims of this village were able to witness the faith and love of Christ as these Christians were tested. The Christians were able to mourn the loss of their loved ones and yet returned good for evil.

My co-worker Ray Thorne and Gary Lane with Christian Broadcasting Network, visited the Church , November 3, 2001, six days after the tragedy. He met with the pastor's wife and wept with her. He let her know that she was not alone, and that many were mourning with her. He shared about other martyrs and widows around the world, and the fellowship of martyrdom that we all had through Jesus Christ. 2 Corinthians 1:3-5: "Blessed be the God and Father of our Lord Jesus Christ, the Father of mercies and God of all comfort, who comforts us in all our affliction so that we may be able to comfort those who are in any affliction with the comfort with which we ourselves are comforted by God. For just as the sufferings of Christ are ours in abundance, so also our comfort is abundant through Christ."

Not long after this massacre I saw pictures of the victims which were taken that day in Pakistan. One unforgettable picture was a little two year girl. Her body lay limp as she was being held up by a man I believed was her father. It was reported that over 30 bullet holes were counted in her tiny body. Angry and disgusted, I wondered what kind of evil person would keep the trigger of a gun down on a two year old child. For three days I struggled with God, with a spirit of vengeance. I was mad. I wanted to get even for this wrong. Why not arm the Christians? I also struggled with God over why He would let this happen. Certainly God was allowing me to feel some of the emotions that the father, mother, brothers and sisters must feel. On the third day, I felt the Lord move on my heart. As if the Lord said to me, "David, the little girl was dead after the first bullet and was safe with Me. I allowed the other 29 bullets to show the violence and death within Islam; in order that Muslims with eyes might see the way of Islam which ultimately leads to violence and death." The Lord really disarmed me when I heard in my spirit, "These Muslim gunmen would never have done this if they had known the love of Jesus." I wept again that day as I was reminded that our fight is not against flesh and blood, but it is a spiritual battle for the hearts and souls, not only of Muslims, but mankind. Our greatest weapon is the gospel of Jesus Christ. This battle will not be won by M-16 guns but by John 3:16 (NIV): "For God so loved the world that he gave his one and only Son, that whoever believes in him shall not perish but have eternal life."

When Christians return love for hate, we bring life out of death. John 12:24:

"Truly, truly, I say to you, unless a grain of wheat falls into the earth and dies, it remains by itself alone; but if it dies, it bears much fruit." The seeds of the martyrs are beginning a harvest in Pakistan as more and more Muslims are coming to Christ every year. Love is conquering the death grip of Islam over the hearts and minds of Muslims. The world cannot understand how the gospel can grow in such a violent environment. They do not understand the words of Jesus, "But you shall receive power when the Holy Spirit has come upon you; and you shall be My witnesses (martyrs) both in Jerusalem, and in all Judea and Samaria, and even to the remotest part of the Earth." (Acts 1:8)

# Part Four: Chapter 16

### Fearless Love: Meditation

Have you ever asked yourself, "Where is God" in the midst of such horrible violence? The answer will always be the same. God is in the same place as when His Son died on the cross. God is love and it is His love that constraints His wrath. God truly loves sinners and wants the unrighteous to be saved. He has blessed his saints with forgiveness of sins, eternal life, supernatural provision, hope, love, joy and peace. God is not satisfied with blessing His followers only; He wants all to be saved. 2 Peter 3:9, "The Lord is not slow about His promise, as some count slowness, but is patient toward you, not wishing for any to perish but for all to come to repentance." God's presence is in His living Church and He suffers with all who suffer. It is His love that motivates His patience so that even the unrighteous might experience His presence and His love. The suffering and the persecution of the Church today is bringing about the repentance of lost souls. Ask God today to save more violent terrorists. Pray that your life would honor the martyrs who have perished by living a life in faithfulness and with love for your enemies.

*Fearless Love Notes:*

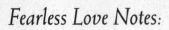
*Fearless Love Notes:*

In 1997 the Russian made Antinopf plane, full of supplies and The Voice of the Martyrs team, flew at a very low altitude across the plains of Sudan. The plane remained low to avoid the radar of the Northern Islamic Government of Sudan. The Government has attacked the Christian population of the south for many years and the death total is estimated at over 2 million.

> They dragged him behind a horse before putting a bullet to his head.

Starvation, nakedness, and the destruction of homes, Churches, roads, water systems, medical support centers and the like are a regular sight in Southern Sudan. The team flew to a village located five miles from the war front. The plane was loaded with food, medicine, blankets, Bibles, and various supplies. These supplies were particularly needed because no direct supply had come to this area in six years. As the plane landed on the narrow overgrown grass runway, hundreds of Sudanese ran out to meet the team. They were so happy to see that believers in Jesus had not forgotten them. Supplies they had prayed for were brought out of the plane for distribution. One of the pastors who met the team was Pastor Abraham. He had the only Bible for his congregation of 400. He shared that this Bible was inherited from his grandfather. He rejoiced as he discovered that the team had brought 400 Bibles for the encouragement of the Christians. Pastor Abraham helped in the distribution of materials, making sure the neediest received help first. He soaked up the fellowship, delighted that Christians from the West had remembered the suffering Sudanese and had come to meet their need.

After the supplies were distributed and a prayer was offered, the team left. It was too dangerous to stay on the ground very long, since the plane may attract attention.

Only four days later GOS (Government of Sudan) soldiers attacked the village. Many homes were burned to the ground, and the Christians that could not escape were shot. The soldiers captured Pastor Abraham. They dragged him behind a horse before putting a bullet to his head. Later the soldiers collected all the Bibles they could find and brought them to the middle of the village, where they soaked them with fuel and burned them.

It is sobering to realize that not only did the soldiers kill Pastor Abraham and other Christians but they collected and destroyed Bibles. Why would military soldiers get involved in Bible collecting? Some contemporary intellectuals argue that the Bible is unreliable and irrelevant. I like to point out to these cynics that if you cannot believe the friends of Jesus, who say that the Bible is powerful, truthful and effective, then believe the enemies of Jesus because they take it dead serious, seriously enough to burn Bibles and kill Christians.

Maybe God allowed the burning of the Bibles in this village so the observers around the world might have a clue as to the deeper problem in Sudan. Sudan's root problem is not tribal, economic or political. It is a spiritual battle!

*Our faith is not worth living for unless it is worth dying for,*

### Truth Worth Dying For

"Our faith is not worth living for unless it is worth dying for," said Jim Elliott famous martyred missionary to the Auca Indians. Religion is not worth dying for if it is just about cultural religion. The root issue involves a fight for Truth. "Jesus answered, 'I am the way, and the truth, and the life. No one comes to the Father except through me.'" (John 14:6 NIV) Truth is worth dying for because the Truth is Jesus! "...you shall know the truth, and the truth shall make you free." (John 8:32) The Truth not only sets you free to live, but free to die. Remember, Truth changes us, we do not change Truth.

I do not believe we know how to live fully, until we learn how to die. When the fear of death is overcome, we have freedom to obey Christ at all cost and enjoy the adventure of a life surrendered to His will.

"Very rarely will anyone die for a righteous man, though for a good man someone might possibly dare to die. But God demonstrates his own love for us in this: While we were still sinners, Christ died for us." (Romans 5:7-8 NIV) Every redeemed child of God has been captured by the dying love of Christ. "We love, because he first loved us." (1 John 4:19) We are called to have that same attitude. "Therefore, since Christ has suffered in the flesh, arm yourselves also with the same purpose, because he who has suffered in the flesh has ceased from sin..." (1 Peter 4:1) Christ does not ask us to do anything He did not accomplish first. He simply invites us to follow in His example.

**Fearless Love: Meditation**

The Bible has been called "God's Love Letter" through the centuries. Jesus himself summarized the teaching of the Bible with love God and love others. (Matthew 22:37-39) Considering that the ultimate message of the Bible is love, why is the Bible so hated, censored, and burned in some places around the world? John 3:19 explains, "This is the judgment, that the Light has come into the world, and men loved the darkness rather than the Light, for their deeds were evil." The natural default of humankind is evil. Love is dangerous because the light of love reveals the evil darkness of hearts. Love sets the oppressed free and brings hope. The oppressors of this world thirst for power. The message of the Bible is a threat to their power because the love of God is more powerful! The message of God sets people free from the fear of oppressors to the freedom of justice and mercy. If you own a Bible today and can read it freely, thank God. Pray that God might make a way for you to help spread Bibles to the Islamic world. Pray that God might give you the joy of giving a Bible directly to a Muslim or non-believer this month.

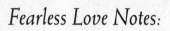

*Fearless Love Notes:*

# THE CROSS:
## Symbol Of What?

While in Sudan I was able to preach one Sunday at a humble Church. The building had dirt floors and the pews were made from mud bricks. Most of the congregation had brought simple crosses made from sticks or pieces of board. The crosses were three to four feet high with an eight to twelve inch cross bar. As the people sang songs, they waved the crosses high in the air worshiping God. Everywhere in Sudan they worship with these simple crosses. After the service I was given a cross by a dear Sudanese woman as a token of love.

I often treasure that scene in my heart. Here Sudanese believers (representing millions of Christians like them) are lifting the cross of Christ in praise and joy while living in a war zone. The more I contemplate the meaning of the cross, the more appropriate I see this expression of faith. Christ conquered sin through suffering and death, and the Sudanese are honoring Jesus' sacrifice, and sharing in His suffering.

In the West, we give crosses to each other to symbolize, friendship, love, hope, and faith. However, we often forget that the cross is still an execution symbol. Can you imagine wearing a cross around your neck or having one on your wall during Roman days? The Romans would have thought you were part of some death cult. A contemporary parallel would be for believers to wear a miniature electric chair around their neck. Non-Christians still see the death that the cross symbolizes. Fundamental Muslims hate the cross. Fundamental Jews hate the cross. Fundamental Hindus hate the cross. Hardened Communists hate the cross. 2 Corinthians 2:15: "For we are a fragrance of Christ to God among those who are being saved and among those who are perishing; to the one an aroma from death to death, to the other an aroma from life to life." It is no surprise that the world persecutes Christians so greatly. We are a threat to their way of life. We smell like death to the world. We are walking signposts, an incense of death. The world does not understand the resurrection that comes through Christ's death on the cross. Death to self is not an attractive feature of the gospel to the unbelieving world. The apostle Paul says in 1 Corinthians 1:23: "but we preach Christ crucified, to Jews a stumbling block, and to Gentiles foolishness..."

### Hatred Of The Cross—Mujahid's story

We saw the hatred of the cross dramatically demonstrated the day my town in Pakistan was burned in 1997. Thousands of Muslims attacked our Christian town because they had been told the lie that the Christians of our area had torn the Qur'an and thrown it into a mosque.

One Imam climbed onto the Churches and broke down the crosses. He tied them to a rope and dragged them through town. As Muslim men were dragging the crosses the Imam followed, hitting the crosses with the bottom of his shoe saying mocking words, "Oh, Jesus if you are alive, strong and mighty come and protect your cross." We learned that this same Imam died of a heart attack during the following week screaming, "The cross is hitting me, the cross is hitting me!"

Christians love the cross because they have experienced the life that comes out of the death of sin and self. Love, joy, and peace fill the new person in Christ. But let us again contemplate the death in which Christ has called us from Scripture:

"He who has found his life shall lose it, and he who has lost his life for My sake shall find it" (Matthew 10:39). "For to me, to live is Christ, and to die is gain" (Philippians 1:21). "For whoever wishes to save his life will lose it; but whoever loses his life for My sake shall find it" (Matthew 16:25). "Now if we have died with Christ, we believe that we shall also live with Him" (Romans 6:8). "For you have died and your life is hidden with Christ in God" (Colossians 3:3).

This death is both spiritual and physical. We spiritually die and are resurrected with Christ the moment we turn away from our sinful nature and receive him by faith. We no longer live for self-gain but for Christ's gain. This death becomes complete the moment we physically die. Our physical bodies must die in order for us to receive our resurrected perfect Heavenly bodies. "The body that is sown is perishable, it is raised imperishable…" (1 Corinthians 15:42).

### Our Personal Cross

The Sudanese believers in Jesus can hold the cross high because they now have great hope. This is not their home. Through Christ their sins are forgiven. They are looking for a better and more lasting resurrection of glory. But I believe they worship with the crosses for yet another reason. There are two crosses to experience. There is the cross of Christ and there is the personal cross we must bear. Again these are the words of Jesus not mine. "If anyone wishes to come after Me, let him deny himself, and take up his cross, and follow Me." (Matthew 16:24). Most

Christians understand the cross of Christ; we have been given salvation through His suffering. Our sins are completely washed and forgiven. Our Father in Heaven is satisfied and we are made perfect. But what about our personal cross we are commanded to bear? Our persecuted brothers and sisters in Christ are our teachers on this issue. Working with the persecuted Church, I have learned that our cross produces the propagation of the gospel and our sanctification.

When others see our difficulties, our economic trials, our marital conflicts, our diseases, persecutions and even our dealing with death; they also see the fruit of the Spirit: Love, joy, peace, patience, kindness, goodness, faithfulness, gentleness and self-control (Galatians 5:22-23). Through this witness, the world catches a glimpse of Christ. When people witness these actions of love surely they wonder how these reactions are not "natural." They seem "supernatural." Through the trials of life we proclaim Christ.

Revelation 12:11 (NIV): "They overcame him by the blood of the Lamb and by the word of their testimony; they did not love their lives so much as to shrink from death." We need to keep in mind how we get a "testimony." First, we must have a "test." Without a test we only have a "moany" (ie moaning!). I think everyone is tired of hearing Christians "moan". The testimonies of believers should be that "they did not love their lives so much as to shrink from death." The spirit of martyrdom keeps every believer faithful until death. We would rather die first than forsake our first love.

# Part Four: Chapter 18

### Fearless Love: Meditation

What does the cross of Christ mean to you? Does it bring emotions of fear or love? Quoted in this chapter is 2 Corinthians 2:15, "For we are a fragrance of Christ to God among those who are being saved and among those who are perishing; to the one an aroma from death to death, to the other an aroma from life to life." Christ has put his Spirit of Martyrdom upon every child of God. Christ's spirit in you has a fragrance. To other living martyrs you are a perfume of life and beauty. To those who are perishing you are a wretched, rank odor of death. Like any perfume it brings no aroma until the seal is broken and the oil released. God has broken the seal of the Church which is Jesus Christ and He pours out the fragrant oil of His saints upon the world. When your pride has been broken and your heart and mind filled with precious oil of Christ's Spirit you are His aroma. Pray that God increases your fragrance with greater dependence on His Spirit. Pray that the olfactory of the Muslim world will awaken to the rich aroma of Christ and His love.

*Fearless Love Notes:*

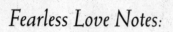
*Fearless Love Notes:*

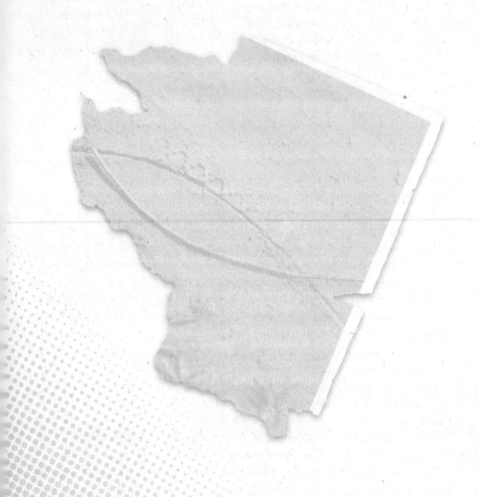

# MARTYRDOM
## In America

United States violent crime rates are among the highest in the world when compared to other developed nations.[i] Escalating violence and terrorism are numbing the American conscience. On October 5, 2006 five Amish girls were martyred because their perpetrator was angry at God. Thirteen-year-old Marian Fisher was the oldest of the Christian children when she stepped forward and asked her killer, "Shoot me first," in an apparent effort to buy the other children time. What's more, Fisher's 11-year-old sister, Barbie, who survived the shooting, allegedly asked the gunman, "Shoot me second."[ii] The courage of their Christian faith was reflected throughout the Amish community. They even reached out with love and forgiveness to the perpetrator's surviving family.

> "Now I have given up on everything else. I have found it to be the only one way to really know Christ and to experience the mighty power that brought Him back to life again, and to find out what it means to suffer and die with Him.

It was amazing to see that America was more captivated by the courage of the Amish girls and the forgiveness of the Amish community than the violence itself. For weeks after this event the newspapers, magazines and television programs focused on the forgiveness that the Amish community offered to the murderer and his family. Some of the Amish community actually cooked meals and visited the perpetrators family and ministered to their needs. This event has become a beacon of hope in the midst of our violence-saturated world.

Cassie Bernall was a 17 year old junior at Columbine High School in Littleton, Colorado. On the morning of April 20, 1999, little did she know this would be the last day of her earthly life. Around 11:00 am she was studying in the library when two fellow classmates stormed in, guns blazing. One of the gunmen confronted Cassie, point blank, and asked the question, "Do you believe in God?" Cassie hesitated for a moment as the barrel of the gun pointed to her head. Suddenly, faith and courage rose somewhere deep inside of her and she answered, "Yes!" At this moment, the bullet released from the chamber and Cassie Bernall was martyred. In this action Cassie witnessed to the gospel to more people than she could have done personally in a hundred life times. Her story is told around the world in places like Iran, Saudi Arabia and others. Thousands, if not tens of thousands of youth have come to know the love and saving grace of Jesus Christ because of her, and the other martyrs of Columbine's story being told.

In a flash Cassie beheld the glory of Christ. She is now eternally in His presence. There is nothing we can offer Cassie to convince her to come back to life here on Earth. Her joy is complete and her satisfaction is beyond measure. She is receiving her reward and has graduated to Heaven with honors.

After the Columbine massacre ended and it was determined that Cassie was dead, her brother entered her room at home and found her personal diary. He began to read beautiful entries from his precious sister. Dated April 18, 1999, she wrote these words, "Now I have given up on everything else. I have found it to be the only one way to really know Christ and to experience the mighty power that brought Him back to life again, and to find out what it means to suffer and die with Him. So, whatever it takes I will be one who lives in the fresh newness of life of those who are alive from the dead." Those are phenomenal words from a girl who had been a Satanist just two years prior. She had hated God and Christians. Something dramatic had obviously happened in her life to cause her to write those words. From Cassie's pen, The Holy Spirit inspired her to leave a record for us; a witness.

When did Cassie Bernall become a martyr? By the evidence of Cassie's own words, the testimony of her life, and the evidence of the Biblical record, she was already a martyr. Cassie illustrated in her death the truth of Jesus' words, "But you shall receive power when the Holy Spirit has come upon you; and you shall be My witnesses both in Jerusalem, and in all Judea and Samaria (and Columbine High), and even to the remotest part of the Earth" (Acts 1:8). Cassie became a martyr (a witness) the day she opened her heart to the love of Christ. The Holy Spirit came to dwell in her heart and filled it with the courageous spirit of martyrdom.

### Christians Will All Die As Martyrs

God knew us before the foundations of this world. He knew our birth, our path of life and he knows the very second of our death. "And as it is appointed for men to die once..." (Hebrews 9:27, NKJV). Mortality is still one hundred percent. Everyone dies. Everyone reading this book has his or her death to face. How are you going to use your death for

God's glory? Or better put, how is God to use your death for His Glory? The good news is that you do not have to worry about it because God already has a plan. There are many ways people die. For some reading this book, God has appointed you to die in a car accident. Some readers are appointed to die from cancer. Some will die peacefully in their sleep, attesting to a long and faithful life. And some readers may have the honor of dying directly for their faith like Cassie Bernall, or Rachel Scott at Columbine High and the host of others who have died for their faith in America and around the world. For those who have the eyes to see, God has ordained the use of the death of every one of his children to die with Christ's spirit of martyrdom; as a witness to His love. If you are a believer in Jesus then God has ordained that you will die for His Glory with a martyr's spirit. In other words, no matter how you die, you will die as a martyr. Your death will be a witness to Christ.

Let me paint a picture for you, as a practical example of what I am saying. Let's say that Joe drives to the store for supplies. On the way to the store a truck hits him in a head-on collision. Joe is killed instantly. As a Christian, the next face Joe sees is the face of his savior, Jesus. At that moment there certainly will be no regrets and only great rejoicing in the presence of Christ and in his realm of perfect love. Joe might even have gratitude that he no longer has to face the pain, rehabilitation and cost involved in surviving the wreck. God's call homeward to Heaven is perfect healing and perfect peace. The suffering and loss in this situation comes to those who survive as they grieve the temporary loss of Joe. Many friends and family will come to the funeral to celebrate Joe's life and mourn their loss. We must keep in mind that funerals are for the survivors not for the dead. One by one, many friends may get up before the audience and say something like this, "Joe, was a faithful man of God. He sacrificed for the good of others, helped those in need, prayed for the sick and worked in the ministry of the Church. He was such a 'witness' of the love of Christ in this community!" Every believer at the funeral will be strengthened in their faith as they consider what God has done through Joe. A hope rises in their hearts as they consider that one day they too will join Joe in Heaven. Last of all, non-believers will come to the funeral to show their respect, through the whole service they will hear and see the gospel of Jesus Christ in action through the testimonies of friends. And through this whole event God gets the glory. The point is God has ordained some to die as a martyr in a car accident for His glory and ultimately our gain.

# Part Four: Chapter 19

I was a youth pastor in Yampa Valley, Colorado for nearly ten wonderful years. One young man whom I knew during this time was Jerod Faucett. At age 13 he was diagnosed with leukemia. He went through radiation therapy sending the cancer into remission for a couple of years. At age 16 it came back with a vengeance. The medical community recommended that he receive a bone marrow transplant as the next step in treating the leukemia. His family moved to Seattle, Washington for four months while Jerod received the bone marrow transplant. During that time my family and I were able to visit Jerod and the Faucett family and witness the beautiful love and faith they all had throughout this trial. After four months the doctors announced that the bone marrow transplant had not worked. There were few options left, so the Faucett family went home to Colorado with the reality that Jerod was going to die soon.

Having moved to work for The Voice of the Martyrs, I again had the privilege of seeing Jerod and his mother in Denver soon after coming home from Seattle. As we sat down to lunch, I realized I was with a seventeen year old high school senior dying of cancer, yet I found that he had peace and even hope in his demeanor. I wanted to probe Jerod's heart and so I asked him, "Jerod, what are you praying for? Are you praying to be healed or are you ready to go home to Jesus?" His answer rang with a peace that only Jesus can give, "I am ready to go home." I looked at Jerod and I said something that I now know was prophetic, "Jerod, you are a martyr and God is going to use your death for his glory." That was the last time I was with Jerod. A few months later he died in the arms of his father and mother. The hospice nurse commented that she had never seen anyone die so peacefully before. Jerod is from the town of Hayden next to Steamboat Springs, Colorado. Hayden's population is 1500 people. His high school student body was just over one hundred students. Yet, over 800 people packed the high school gym for his funeral and heard the testimony of Christ in his life. I believe Jerod died as a martyr. The witness of his life and family has touched thousands around the world.

God has also ordained that some of us will die for the direct witness of our faith. When confronted with violence and asked to deny our faith we will experience that supernatural peace and courage. "Never will I leave you, never will I forsake you, so we say with confidence, the Lord is my helper; I will not be afraid. What can man do to me?" (Hebrews 13:5-6). "Death has been swallowed up in victory. Where, O death, is your victory? Where, O death, is your sting?" (1 Corinthians 15:54, 55). Ultimately, death for every believer is the diploma of life as they receive the goal and the hope of their soul, enjoying the glory, beauty and peace of God for eternity.

If you are in Christ today and have His Holy Spirit dwelling in you, then you also have a martyr's spirit. You get to live as a martyr and die as a martyr and one day those around you, if not the world, will recognize it. God gives you a choice. Are you willing to surrender in your faith to the spirit of loving martyrdom? And are you willing to live for Christ, no longer fearing death? The reality is that God already has your death planned and will use it for his glory but your surrender will determine how much you enjoy the journey of getting there.

### The Freedom Of Martyrdom

The Holy Spirit wants you to surrender every part of your life to His loving care and control. As the saying goes, "the two things in life that you cannot avoid, are death and taxes." Today God is calling you to surrender your death. (I know most people would rather surrender their taxes!) God does not want you to live in the fear of suffering and death. The Bible says, "Since the children have flesh and blood, he too shared in his humanity so that by his death he might destroy him who holds the power of death—that is, the devil—and free those who all their lives were held in slavery by their fear of death" (Heb 2:14). God has our death under his control, but the fear of death keeps people enslaved. Christ came that we might be free. And those who are in Christ Jesus are free indeed.

### Freedom In Sweet Surrender

When we live in Christ's power and love without fear of death we find freedom. As Mujahid and I have given this message in hundreds of places we have seen thousands of believers respond in sweet surrender to the spirit of martyrdom. As a physical gesture of a spiritual decision we have asked believers in these auditoriums around the world to stand if they were surrendered as martyrs and wanted to be found faithful unto death. In most places we have seen the majority of the audience stand. Around the world believers are trusting God fully with their death and their life. Consequently, these believers are fearless and enjoying the journey of life. Because martyrs are not ruled by fear, God can use them for anything. The adventure begins as we lay aside our control and trust His voice in leading our lives and our death.

God is asking you to give over your fear of your own death to Him. The end of terrorism starts when fear flees from your heart so that peace can reign. Right now I invite you to say a prayer of surrender that thousands of others have uttered. "Father, I surrender my death to you! No matter how I die, I trust you for the time, place, and event of my death. Use it for your glory and my gain. I thank you that you have made me a martyr for love. I get to die as a loving martyr and until then, live as a loving martyr. As I have surrendered my death so I surrender my life. Find me faithful today. Help me to love all those who you put in my path. Help me to support believers suffering persecution and martyrdom around the world and especially in the Islamic world. Give me opportunities to show Muslims what a true martyr is: A loving faithful servant of Christ. May the surrender of my life and death be the reward of the suffering of Christ and His Body around the world. I pray all this for your divine glory, Amen."

If you have just prayed that prayer I believe applause is breaking forth in Heaven. You have surrendered to love and to be a faithful vessel of love no matter what the cost. Love is the ultimate banner of the Christian. It is how the world will know us; it is how Muslims will be transformed by us.

The Christian martyrs are bringing a death blow to Islam. In every Islamic nation in the world God has planted his martyrs. They are seeds of love, faith and courage. They are transforming hearts, from enmity and hatred towards Jews, Buddhist, Hindus, and Christians, to becoming hearts full of love for all people everywhere. Love conquers all! The ultimate expression of love is self-sacrifice for the good of others. Islam is crumbling because darkness flees with the first rays of sun. The Son of righteousness is rising with healing in His wings in the Muslim world. Everyday tens and hundreds of Muslims are surrendering their lives to Christ. That number will turn into thousands daily as the martyrs of love continue to grow.

As you are a faithful Christian martyr you are doing something in your own nation that Christian martyrs in Islamic nations cannot do. As they are faithful in their own land, they are doing something you cannot do. Together we build the Kingdom of God.

In Part Five we will look at the freedom and confidence we can have as martyrs. Recognizing that our death is under the complete control and plan of God and therefore we have freedom to accomplish everything God requires of us. We will see how God protects our lives and how true safety is living by faith in Christ.

**Fearless Love: Meditation**

The creation of the world teaches us about the spirit of martyrdom. Romans 1:20 says, "For his invisible attributes, namely, his eternal power and divine nature, have been clearly perceived, ever since the creation of the world, in the things that have been made. So they are without excuse." A general law of biology is life begets life. A mother sacrifices part of her body to bring forth a new baby. The new baby takes nutrients, minerals, energy and even pain to bring into this world. Sometimes mothers die in childbirth. As we grow, plants offer their life for our ingestion. Animals provide us with meat at the sacrifice of their lives. Dogs have been known to fight until death in protection of their masters. A mother bear will risk its life in protection of her cub. The heroes of history are those who have given much of themselves for the betterment of society. God has designed life to work noblest when given for the life of creation. We live in greatest abundance when we are working within the design for our lives. What are you giving your life to today? How do you see Christ's spirit of martyrdom working in your family, work, friends, community? Pray that the martyrs of Islam will have their eyes opened to God's creation message that martyrdom was made for love and not violence.

# Part Four: Chapter 19

## Part 4 Group Discussion And Contemplation

Pray: Ask God to give insight into God's purposes for His children in death.

*Optional Audio Book: Play Disc 2, Track 21-22,*
*Hatred Of The Cross—for five minutes*

Pastor Emanuel would not dishonor the Word of God by throwing it down to the carpet. What issues of faith are you willing to die for? What issues of faith can you compromise?

Saint Paul was a terrorist against followers of Christ until Jesus changed his life. He recorded these words in Acts 22:4(ESV) "I persecuted this Way to the death, binding and delivering to prison both men and women..." What do you think of the chances of a terrorist like Paul coming to faith in Jesus today? If some of the Apostles of old came from terrorist backgrounds does this give you hope for turning around the lives of modern terrorists today? What will it take for terrorist to hear the good news of Jesus Christ? How can we get this message to them?

What do you think of the statement, "This battle will not be won by M-16 guns but by John 3:16?" Discuss the implementation of this quote.

Do you believe this is a true statement? "If you cannot believe the friends of Christ then believe the enemies of Christ because the gravity of their violence against the gospel brings credibility to the message." Why or why not?

In Sudan an unknown number of Christians have died as the fundamental Islamic government has tried to squash the witness of the gospel. Yet by all indications this force has caused the gospel to spread more. Have you seen others fight against something only to make it worse like putting water on an oil fire? Share one experience and tell what happened.

Think about the statement, "Our faith is not worth living for unless it is worth dying for," How does this statement make you feel? Is this statement Biblical? Why or why not.

Name all the cultural ideas the cross symbolizes. What does the symbol of a cross mean to you?

Is the crucifixion of Christ on the cross an action of mercy or justice? Why? When Christians take up their crosses are they practicing mercy or justice? Why?

Why is the cross of Christ a symbol of both hope and offense to the Muslim world?

Do living martyrs offer hope to the violence in the United States and other nations? Why or why not?

How do you think the Christian martyrs in America(Marian Fisher, Rachel Scott, Cassie Barnell), since 1999 and the Colombine High school shooting in Colorado have changed the way people think of Christians and martyrdom?

## Part Four: Chapter 19

What do you think of the statement, "You will die as a martyr…God is going to use your death for His glory?" Can you think of some Biblical verses that either support that statement or refute it?

Do you believe that you are going to die as a martyr? Why or why not?

**Witness:** Read the obituary this week. Consider the impact the individuals have made through their life and death. Read about a soldier or leader who recently was killed. What can you learn from his life and death? See if there are ways that you can honor the death of the faithful witnesses and even minister to their loved ones. Pray that you can have a conversation via the internet or in person with a Muslim regarding jihad and martyrdom and how Christ calls us to be martyrs of love.

**Personal Application:** Think about your death this week. Visit a graveyard. If you were to die soon what legacy would you leave to your loved ones and your community? Are you living a life without regrets? Ask God to reveal the areas in your life that you need to change and begin to make changes as they come to mind. If the fear of death haunts you ask God to give you more faith and begin to renew your mind with scriptures to overcome your fear.

**Digging Deeper:** Read portions of Foxes Book of Martyrs on the internet or purchase one from www.SpiritofMartyrdom.com

**Ending Prayer:** Pray through the points and insights that you gained.

### Fearless Love: Endnotes

i   *http://en.wikipedia.org/wiki/Crime_in_the_United_States*

ii  *http://abcnews.go.com/US/story?id=2531138&CMP=OTC-RSSFeeds0312*

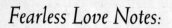
*Fearless Love Notes:*

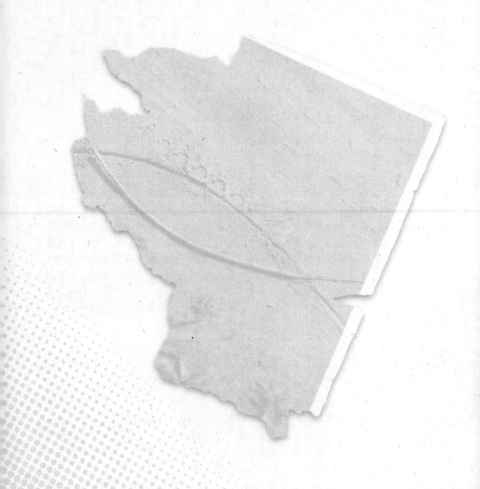

# BOMBING
## *Of Baghdad*

> God gave Musa incredible peace in his heart in the midst of the chaos.

Another bomb rocked the prison cell. The concussion from the blast seemed to shake the foundations. This constant bombardment had given the prisoners little sleep for two straight weeks. The political prisoners in Baghdad, Iraq had heard the guards talk about how the American bombs were accurately destroying Saddam Hussein's government buildings. The prisoners were all locked up in downtown Baghdad beside Iraq's Department of Interior. This was one of the major government buildings in Baghdad. The prisoners knew that it would only be a matter of time before this building was hit and all the prisoners were killed. No one was quite sure why, but many of the prisoners had been moved to this particular prison right before the war. They were overcrowded. A large room for a prison, about 20 feet wide by 30 feet long, this cell was now tight in space with 50 inmates. Every night for the past two weeks had been the same. As the bombing started the prisoners would pack together in the bathroom, like sardines in a can because it was the securest place in the cell.

In the midst of this chaos one man distinguished himself as a leader. His name was Musa. He was darker skinned than most of the Iraqis because he was a foreigner. There was a confidence about him. While the nerves of the inmates were frayed and tempers flared, Musa seemed to be the one who continued to bring peace back to the cell. He was the only Christian among Muslim Iraqi inmates.

Musa had been arrested Feb 1, 2003 with six other house Church leaders. Saddam's secret police did not like the idea that these house Church pastors were meeting in homes and witnessing to Muslims. Some Muslims converted and became Christians. Even though Musa was only in his late thirties he had the most prison experience among the house Church pastors. He had been arrested multiple times for his Christian faith and work. Five times in Eritrea he was put in prison for preaching the gospel and leading Bible studies. Then he traveled to Sudan and started house Churches. After Sudan the Lord led him to Jordan where he encouraged believers and started more house Churches. He was arrested in Jordon. After his imprisonment a pastor prophesied to Musa that God was calling him to go to Iraq. For two years he had lived and ministered in Iraq.

The rest of the Iraqi house Church pastors were released after one month on March 1st just before the war began. But Musa was kept in prison and then was moved to the Department of Interior prison right before the war. After the war started and the bombs were falling, Musa was able to minister to the hearts of the Iraqi Muslims. He continued to share the Gospel with them. Musa knew the voice of God and the Lord had spoken to him that he would not die in prison. Musa told the inmates that as long as he was in prison, the Department of Interior would not be bombed. God gave Musa incredible peace in his heart in the midst of the chaos. He boldly shared "do not be afraid, God has more plans for me to share the gospel with others!"

During the war, American and Allied troops bombed nearly every major government building in Baghdad except the Department of Interior. Musa and all the prisoners were released the day Baghdad fell and it was the American soldiers who opened the doors of the cell. Now we know, as Paul Harvey says, "the rest of the story."

I recently visited Musa and other believers in Iraq. While in Baghdad, I heard three to ten bombs explode every day from Islamic insurgents. Gun battles are a constant background noise day and night. Two different nights gun battles raged outside the door of the ministry center where I was staying with Musa. Most nights I went to bed with gun shots ringing in the distance. One night after praying for a sick Church member, one of the house Church leaders was shot in the arm while walking home to the ministry center. In the midst of this violence I never felt fear. I was amazed at the peace God gave me. My faith has been strengthened through the years by sisters and brothers like Musa. Many of our persecuted brothers and sisters live with a confidence in God's provision and protection. They live each day as if they are indestructible.

**Fearless Love: Meditation**

Musa has an amazing testimony. He would never have experienced the supernatural provision of God if he would not have been arrested and persecuted. David Witt would never have heard Musa's story if he was not willing to trust God's protection during his visit to Iraq. The key function of a living martyr is trust. Without trust a relationship with God is not possible. Hebrews 11:6, "And without faith it is impossible to please him..." The greater the measure of trust becomes the greater the sense of adventure. Worry and anxiety melt away as a mind is put upon the faithful, loving oversight of God. Let your worries go today and put them into the loving hands of God. Thank God that He is using conflict with the Islamic world to build faith and strengthen His Church.

*Fearless Love Notes:*

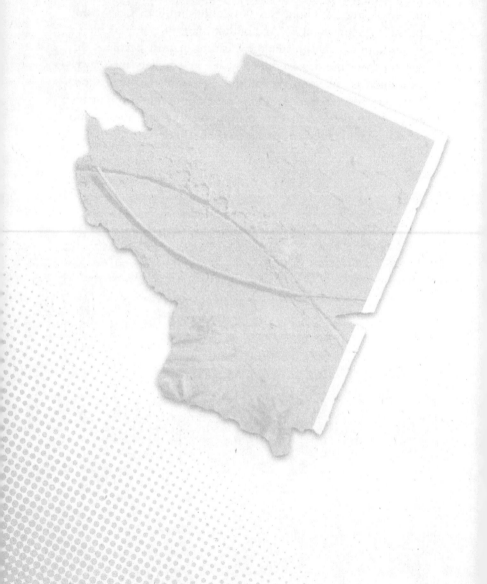

# GOD HAS ORDAINED
## Our Days

In Psalm 139:16 it says, "All the days ordained for me were written in your book before one of them came to be." God is not going to add one second nor will He subtract one second. He knows our choices. He knows our future. He knows our death. All is planned. Believers have great peace because we know God is in control and using all circumstances for His glory and our gain. The sovereignty of God is the pillow at night on which every Christian rests their head.

I have shared with Muslims that I cannot die. I am indestructible until that perfect day in which God will take me home. God has ordained the exact moment I am to die. When that moment comes, why fight the will of God? I am going to a better place and with no regrets by the

> **I have shared with Muslims
> that I cannot die.**

grace of God. I do not need to know the time and day. The timing is God's problem. I am called to enjoy the journey, trusting God each step of the way, walking in perfect obedience, which gives me a childlike fearlessness.

God's word is clear. We are not to test the Lord our God, and foolishness and disobedience lead to difficulty. God is not mocked; a person reaps what he sows. But a believer with a pure heart who is seeking God in obedience has nothing to be anxious about. A righteous person's steps are ordered and in the difficulties of their life God will develop character and maturity.

### Indestructible Attitude

With God's grace Christians walk with a peace and a calling from God. Every step of the journey is significant! Tom White, The Voice of the Martyrs Executive Director, shared how in Vietnam he asked a Vietnamese Christian how they have endured such suffering of persecution through all these years. She answered, "Persecution is not suffering, but disobedience to God is true suffering." This believer has an indestructible attitude. Her steps are ordained by God and each one has its purpose. When we have peace with God and understand his calling we can endure all things. We are participating in the divine nature of God.

Job 14:5 (NIV): "Man's days are determined, you have decreed the number of his months and have set limits he cannot exceed." God is the master designer. Nothing has escaped his perfect plan.

Dr. PP Job runs the ministry founded by Richard Wurmbrand in India. Dr. Job is an evangelist and once a year holds gospel outreaches in large cities of India. These gatherings range from twenty thousand to half a million people in outside arenas. One year as an outreach was about to begin, tens of thousands were gathered to hear the preaching of the gospel. Dark rain clouds raced towards the city and the rain seemed imminent. Thousands of dollars had been spent for the event and representatives had flown in from around the world. The crowd was growing anxious and beginning to stand and gather their belongings to vacate. The outreach was on the verge of disaster. Suddenly Richard Wurmbrand came to the microphone. He announced that everyone should sit down. "It will not rain," he assured them. He went on to say that he was a Jew, and as a Jew he had learned to be frugal and waste no money. He reminded everyone that Jesus was also a Jew. Jesus was the Lord of this whole event. He owned it all. Jesus spent thousands of dollars on this event and He would not let it rain. The people sat back down and the service continued. During the outreach it rained all over the city but it did not rain on the arena. As soon as the event was over and people began to file home, the Heavens opened and it began to pour. Richard Wurmbrand had an indestructible attitude. God's work cannot be thwarted.

"So teach us to number our days, that we may present to You a heart of wisdom" (Psalm 90:12). A wise person learns to number his days. Why? Because every day has significance. God does not waste His resources. He has counted every day for maximum yield. Every day Christians can mark off another day on their calendar and, with great hope, think, "praise God, one more day closer to His glory." Mathematics is an exact science in the universe. God is the ultimate accountant. Everything has its place and purpose.

Pastor Wurmbrand had come to understand that God never wasted His resources. Each person and event has been carefully calculated for maximum yield. Every person's life has a great significance no matter how insignificant it may seem. One pastor friend, Randy Sutter, put it this way, "You are like a hundred dollar bill in the pocket of God. Every penny he has planned and he will spend you perfectly for his divine glory." As we grow in trusting God's character, we have great peace and satisfaction in trusting his sovereign hand.

A Jewish Rabbi once said, "Coincidence is an unkosher word, there is not a good Hebrew translation and you cannot find that word in your Old Testament Bible." There are no accidents with God! What comfort we can have as we sometimes feel insignificant, and life seems out of control. "Are not two sparrows sold for a penny? Yet not one of them will fall to the ground apart from the will of your Father. And even the very hairs of your head are all numbered. So don't be afraid; you are worth more than many sparrows." (Matthew 10:29 NIV)

### Fearless Love: Meditation

There is a joke about a smart man and a dense man watching a horse race on television. The smart man says I bet you one hundred dollars that horse in lane four wins. The dense man agrees to the bet. Horse four wins the race and the smart man laughs in his triumph and admits that this race was a rerun and he had watched it on television the day before. The dense man replied that he also had seen the race the day before but figured there was little chance that horse four could win two days in a row. A martyr's confidence comes from faith that the all powerful and all loving God has the future in complete control. Isaiah 26:3, "You keep him in perfect peace whose mind is stayed on you, because he trusts in you." Whatever a person loves he or she will trust. Who are you trusting- yourself, friends, society, government, or God? Pray for God to raise your confidence in His providential hand. Pray for the global Body of Christ that believers in Jesus increase in an indestructible attitude.

*Fearless Love Notes:*

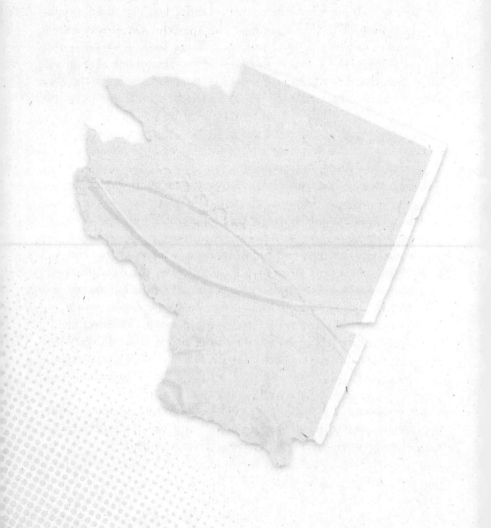

# GOD
## Is Fully Sovereign

A scared and panicked man introduced himself as the gunman. He wanted to know if Paul was some holy man.

God is not ninety-nine percent sovereign. He is one hundred percent sovereign or He is not sovereign at all. Freedom, joy, peace are all released and experienced as we understand this in our mind and trust God's full control in our heart. As soon as we surrender completely to his control in all things we can begin to enjoy the journey of life. Proverbs 31 says of the excellent women, "She smiles at the future." Believers who surrender to God's control do not have terror at what the future might bring, but a beautiful anticipation of the adventure of life.

In Bangladesh, I was sitting in a bungalow with a grass ceiling where there were fans rotating to help us stay cool in the ninety degree humid heat. Sitting with me was a dear Bangladeshi in his sixties whom I will call Paul. He is loved by children, adults and the elderly. He has helped Bangladeshis to understand the gospel. Under his leadership thousands of Muslims have responded to the gospel. He has helped them find shelter, food, a job, and education as many of them have been persecuted for their new faith, kicked out of their villages and made homeless and hungry. Through the years Paul has become an object of great persecution himself.

He shared with me how he had been beaten thirty-two times, twenty times there have been attempts to take his life. God spared his life every time. He shared one of the attempted murders with me.

One day he was alone sitting at his desk when suddenly a man burst into the office. He was holding a gun at his side. He ran up to Paul at the desk with the obvious intent to shoot him. The next moment Paul saw a look of terror and bewilderment on the face of the attacker. The attacker screamed and as quickly as he had entered the office he turned and ran out. Ten minutes later Paul's phone rang. A scared and panicked man introduced himself as the gunman. He wanted to know if Paul was some holy man. Without prompting the man began to pour out all the details of the event. He had been promised the equivalent of a thousand dollars by a local Imam (Muslim cleric) for the murder of Paul. He had already received five hundred dollars. When he came into the office suddenly his arm became paralyzed, he could not lift the gun. As he spoke on the phone, he still could not raise his arm. He knew it had to be God who was protecting his intended victim. He asked if Paul could help his arm to be restored. Paul told him that he could help. He prayed for the gunman and the gunman's arm was immediately restored. Paul went on to share the gospel with him. Today this gunman is a Christian and a leader in the Church.

Paul has experienced great trial and difficulty in his life; yet I find him to be a man of extreme humility, joy, faith, and hope. He has an indestructible attitude and he is enjoying the adventure of trusting and serving Christ.

### Fearless Believer In Iran

In Iran the gospel is growing. An Iranian contact tells me that by their ministry and network of believers in Iran they are seeing an average of four to five hundred Iranian Muslims respond to the gospel every month. One Iranian has been traveling the countryside of Iran preaching the gospel in villages publicly. In one village square where he was preaching, the police arrested him and wanted to scare him out of preaching the gospel any further. They told him that if they caught him preaching again they would throw him into prison with the violent and evil men that they had locked up. A big smile came to the Iranian believer's face and he told the police what a privilege it would be because Jesus had told him to preach the gospel to everyone and especially the sinners and those in prison. He went on to say, "I am sure that those criminals have never heard the gospel even once. Oh, please may it be so that I can spend time with these inmates and explain the gospel carefully to them." The police were not happy with this answer.

They told him. "Since you want to be with the other prisoners, we will not lock you up with them but we will put you into solitary confinement. You will rot in prison alone!" The Iranian believer responded, "Oh, you have no idea how wonderful that sounds to me! You see a few years ago when I first gave my life to Jesus, I would hike a tall mountain and spend hours alone with Jesus. Those were some of the most precious times in my life and I have been so busy preaching and traveling this past year that I am missing time alone with Him." The police were now enraged from their failure to scare him. "You do not understand the seriousness of this situation and the power we hold. If you do not stop preaching we will kill you! We can kill you and no one will ever know what happened to you!" Again the Iranian believer responded, "Praise be to God, to live is Christ to die is gain, the moment you kill me the next face I see will be my Jesus. Do you think you might kill me today? I am ready to go home to Jesus!" The police decided that he was crazy and told him to leave the police station.

This Iranian believer illustrated the same attitude as Saint Paul in 2 Corinthians 5:6-8: "Therefore, being always of good courage, and knowing that while we are at home in the body we are absent from the Lord—for we walk by faith, not by sight—we are of good courage, I say, and prefer rather to be absent from the body and to be at home with the Lord."

If you do not stop preaching we will kill you! We can kill you
and no one will ever know what happened to you!

### Ministers of Humility

All these believers have found the joy of humility. Their trust is fully in God and the identity they have been given in Christ. Biblical humility is seeing yourself the way God sees you. I like to define it this way: Humility is not thinking highly of yourself, nor is it thinking lowly of yourself, it is the freedom to not have to think of yourself. These believers have died to themselves and now live an abundant life in Christ. Their thoughts, actions and lives belong to Jesus. Galatians 2:20: "I have been crucified with Christ and I no longer live, but Christ lives in me." This is a true spirit of martyrdom. Martyrs have been crucified with Christ which is past tense. So if the old man no longer lives, who is living today in your body? Jesus Christ! We trust God's word by faith. A dead man cannot have thoughts for himself. Therefore, true humility is taking the thoughts of Christ captive.

### No Closed Nations For Martyrs

With faith like the examples just described, Christians can begin to understand why the gospel is growing today in every Muslim nation in the world. The national believers in those nations are indestructible; they will not die until God has completed his plan for their lives. Jesus says in Matthew 16:18 (ESV), "I will build my Church, and the gates of

# Part Five: Chapter 22

Hell shall not prevail against it."

Some nations are considered "closed" to the gospel of Jesus Christ. For the last 2000 years the gospel has spread, and grown throughout "closed" nations. What some people do not understand is that there are no "closed" nations to the gospel for martyrs.

A few years ago, Tom White in an editorial for the VOM newsletter illustrated this point with a story of a farmer and a scarecrow. A farmer puts up scare crows in his fields to scare birds away from the crop. Yet, a smart bird learns that scare crows are only sign posts declaring, "Over here, the food is very plentiful!" The Islamic governments that threaten, persecute, and have laws against preaching Christ are scare crows. But scare crows have no real power. The smart Christian begins to recognize scare crows as sign posts that invite him to the harvest of souls. Today, many smart Christian birds are flocking to the Muslim harvest.

God is calling each one of us to have wisdom like the smart birds. Islamic terrorist have only weapons of fear, hatred and violence. They are sign posts. Islam is crumbling under a greater force. The force of God's love being poured out by indestructible Christian martyrs. God is calling us to put on the mind of Christ, which is to become a smart bird with an indestructible attitude. We must have a fearless love that seeks only to be obedient to our Father in Heaven.

### Fearless Love: Meditation

With the love and grace of Jesus Christ in our lives, life and death is a win/win scenario. The Muslim Background Believer from Iran had a win/win faith. He trusted God to use the policemen as instruments of God's hand. He saw God's purpose if he was put in prison with other inmates. He saw the opportunity if put in solitary confinement and he saw the ultimate victory if they were to kill him. The Iranian believer could not lose and the police finally gave up. God has called you to win/win faith. "For to me, to live is Christ, and to die is gain" (Philippians 1:21). Are there areas of your life where God has been calling you to greater faith? List them and pray for grace to obey and start living by faith. Apply a win/win attitude today and surrender your fear. Now ask God to help you take the mind of Christ captive. Pray that many Muslims begin to seek the win/win life of faith in Jesus Christ.

## Part 5 Group Discussion And Contemplation

Pray: Ask God to give insight into a fearless attitude of suffering and death.

*Optional Audio Book: Play Disc 3, Track 8 and 9,*
*God Is Fully Sovereign—for six minutes*

It can be said that the person with the most confidence usually begets leadership. Musa's confidence in God during imprisonment helped him minister God's character to others. When is confidence reckless and when is it serving? Do you remember a time you felt God gave you confidence in a difficult trial? What happened?

Musa has been in prison seven times. Does this make his faith in Christ more credible? In what areas of life are you credible because of your experiences?

Musa "knew the voice of God" and God promised that Musa would not die in prison. Could God have protected Musa's life without telling him so? What do God's children "hearing" the voice of God tell us about the character of God? How do we know when we hear God's voice and not another voice?

David Witt experienced God's peace in the midst of gun battles and bombs. Why does God give peace in the midst of chaos? Have you experienced God's peace in the midst of danger before? What happened?
What do you think of the statement that "Christians are indestructible?" Is this foolish thinking or Biblically minded? Can you think of some Biblical stories or verses that support or refute this statement?

# Part Five: Chapter 22

What do you think the statement means? "Persecution is not suffering, but disobedience to God is true suffering." How do we suffer when we are disobedient to God?

Think about the idea that God is the ultimate accountant. How is your spiritual balance statement looking? If you were in God's place how would you "spend" your life?

Why did "Paul" of Bangladesh pray for the healing of the attempted assassin? This act of compassion towards his assailant tells us what about the character of Paul? What does it tell us about Christ?

The Iranian believer rejoiced in the persecution from the police. How was he able to have such joy at every difficult scenario they offered? Why do you think the police finally gave up? What did the police really want to accomplish in the life of this Iranian believer?

What do you think of the statement, "Humility is not thinking highly of yourself, nor is it thinking lowly of yourself, it is the freedom to not have to think of yourself?" Is this a Biblical Truth? What verses of scriptures can you think of to support or refute this statement?

Who are the scare crows threatening the proclamation of Jesus Christ today? If the terrorist opposing the gospel are really only scare crows what is holding back many Christians from freely sharing their faith in Jesus Christ?

**Witness:** Stretch your faith this week and seek out someone in need. Determine to help meet their needs while sharing the Gospel of Jesus Christ with them. If possible seek out a Muslim and let them know that you do not believe there are any accidents and you want to be their friend because of what Jesus Christ has done in your life.

**Personal Application:** If you were totally convinced of God's sovereignty in your life would you do some things different? Why? Is God calling you to take greater steps of faith in some areas of your life? Ask God to increase your confidence in His provision.

**Digging Deeper:** Read from the Bible the book of Amos chapter 3, Daniel chapter 2 and Revelation chapter 1 and think about the implications of God's sovereignty from these chapters.

**Ending Prayer:** Pray through the points and insights that you gained.

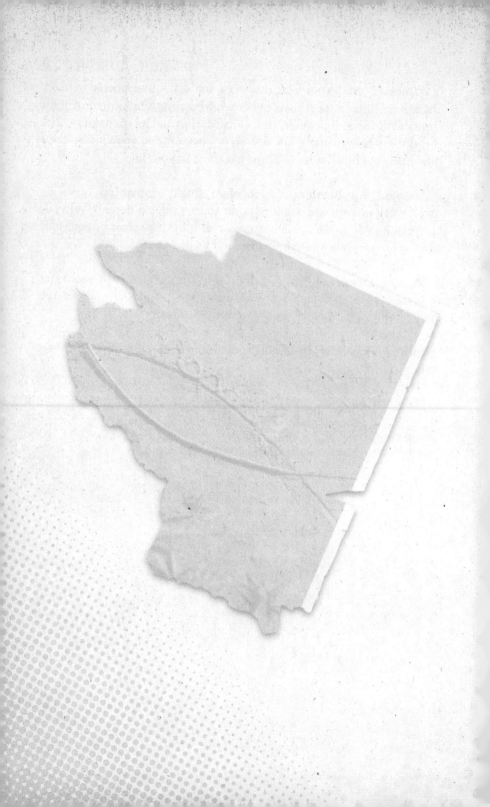

*Fearless Love Notes:*

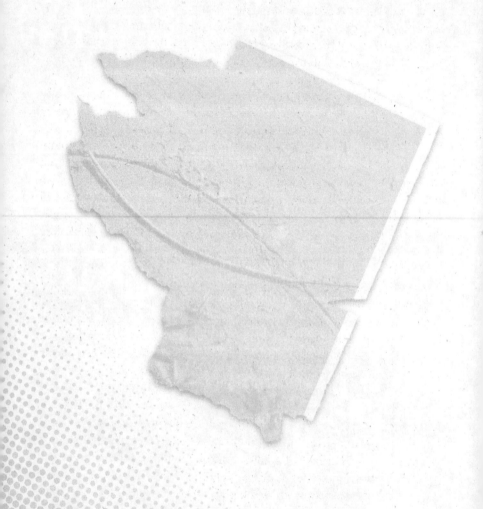

# THE GREAT
*Debate*

The incentive of martyrdom for jihad is Paradise. There is a great debate within the Islamic world today regarding the 9/11 suicide Muslim martyrs on whether they were rewarded with Paradise or Hell. Most Muslims believe that they are in Paradise although they are reluctant to share this belief with non-Muslims. In public Muslims admit that they do not know the eternal destination of these Muslims. This is a safe answer and theologically correct within Islamic doctrine since no one can know the ultimate judgment of Allah regarding Paradise or Hell.

Yet in the midst of this debate there is a minority of devout and liberal Muslims who are trying to make a case that jihad should only be applied in spiritual manners and not in physical violence. The challenge to this group of Islamic reformers is that the Qur'an and the history of Islam and orthodox doctrine of Islam directly support violent struggle. Fundamental Muslims claim that Islamic reformers (liberal Muslims) are not true Muslims.

## Paradise for Islamic Martyrs

Today around the world in mosques, books and media, fundamental Islamic teachers are calling Muslims to join the struggle "jihad" within the community of Islam against the non-believers. The fundamental teachers preach that jihad is the way of Islam and the most rewarded deed within Islam. They quote from the Qur'an and the Hadith to support their cry. The martyrs will have all their bad deeds forgiven and will be able to intercede for seventy family members. They show that the martyrs will obtain Paradise and eternal blissful sex. Within Islamic doctrine Paradise is the enjoyment of all the pleasures of the flesh including what is forbidden on Earth. In Paradise nothing is forbidden. Martyrs will receive extravagant castles; food of every kind beyond measure; alcohol will be served without end. They will be given seventy-two eternal virgins. Their bodies will be virulent and will have the sexual strength of over seventy men. This will allow for constant sexual indulgence. Every imaginable sexual experience will be allowed and enjoyed.

# Part Six: Chapter 23

### Muslim Women Martyrs

Islamic scholars admit that it is unclear regarding the rewards for women who die in behalf of Islam. This creates some tension since the male sexual experience within Paradise is so dominant. It is not propagated by respected Islamic scholars that women will receive seventy-two naked virgin males with whom they will have continuous sex. Most people agree that this offer is not as attractive to women. What is agreed among Muslims is that Allah honors the women martyrs with great blessings. They will receive the finest goods of Paradise, comfort, security and all these in abundance.

It is clear within the Islamic world that the reward of Paradise is the motivation of Muslim martyrs. The carrot of Paradise continues to increase zeal for jihad and the growing fundamentalism. Unless there is a major shift away from the teaching of the reward of martyrs within Islam, the world will continue to experience escalation in suicide bombings, terrorism and wars.

Islam and Biblical Christianity are similar in that both reward martyrdom. However, the type of reward and the motivation are quite different. A Muslim martyr is motivated by violence and power to propagate Islam. A Christian martyr is motivated by love to bless others. Islamic martyrdom is bringing suffering and loss to your enemies to gain favor before Allah in order to enter Paradise. Christian martyrdom calls for personal suffering and loss for the benefit of your enemy. Christian Martyrdom is not to assure a place in Heaven. According to the Bible, as believers in Jesus Christ, we already have a special place prepared for us in Heaven.

**Fearless Love: Meditation**

A living martyr was working day and night serving the needs of others and was asked how they lived so selflessly. He answered, "You esteem me wrong. God will reward me greatly for all this labor. I am not working just for the benefit of others but also for myself." Who are you working for today? God allows us the choice of how much reward we receive here on earth or we defer it for eternal life . The rewards in heaven will last much longer and come with greater satisfaction as you are motivated by the love of Christ. Colossians 3:23-24 (ESV): "Whatever you do, work heartily, as for the Lord and not for men, knowing that from the Lord you will receive the inheritance as your reward. You are serving the Lord Christ." Pray that God will help you work for a lasting reward. Pray that the eyes of Muslims are open to discover that they have a Father in heaven who wants to reward them for becoming martyrs of love instead of hate.

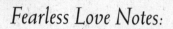

*Fearless Love Notes:*

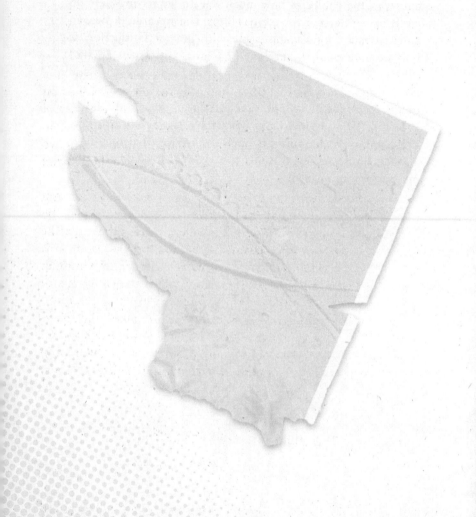

# BIBLICAL REWARDS
*In Heaven*

Rewards in Heaven may be one of the most exciting doctrines within Scripture that is often overlooked or misunderstood among Christians. The New American Standard Bible uses the word "reward" 25 times in the New Testament. These references teach about the rewards of God for His children. One of the classic quoted verses of the Bible is Hebrews 11:6 (ESV): "And without faith it is impossible to please him, for whoever would draw near to God must believe that he exists and that he rewards those who seek him." Most of the time this verse is quoted in the context of faith and little attention is given to the rewards that God has stored up for those who seek him. But Hebrews 11:6 illustrates two essential precepts of faith that pleases God. One is that God exists and second is that He rewards those who seek him.

By my experience and study there is a historical void in a thorough doctrine and teaching regarding rewards. While rewards may be mentioned occasionally it is usually in vague terms and without specific definitions. This may be from the concern that the inference of rewards breeds confusion regarding salvation as earned. Historical Christian doctrine is that salvation is a gift of God and never earned by acts of righteousness. Salvation is received from God by faith alone!

A careful study regarding rewards in the Bible undoubtedly shows that rewards are never connected with salvation. Rewards are always in relationship with the judgment of God regarding our faithfulness in living righteously because of our gift of salvation and new life in Christ

*Jesus encourages believers to seek rewards in Heaven.*

Jesus. Consider Matthew 6:1: "Beware of practicing your righteousness before men to be noticed by them; otherwise you have no reward with your Father who is in Heaven." Rewards are given in the context of the father heart of God. God as a Father desires to honor and reward his children. Matthew 6:1 warns the children of God against pride and the consequences are losing your reward in Heaven, but not Heaven itself. Inferred in this verse and directly supported in 1 Corinthians 3:15 is that there will be some in Heaven with few rewards.

There is no doubt that our acts of righteousness do matter. In fact, the very last chapter of the Bible emphasizes this point, Revelation 22:12 "Behold, I am coming quickly, and My reward is with Me, to render to every man according to what he has done." God has given us the free gift of eternal life. Now every believer can serve God back with good works of service. These acts of service do impact our future. The Bible shows us that there is continuity between this life and the next. While our deeds do not affect our salvation they do shape our future experience in Heaven. The future expectation of appearing before the Lord gives every Christian greater motivation to live a life of obedience, holiness and significance.

Jesus encourages believers to seek rewards in Heaven. Matthew 6:19-20: "Do not store up for yourselves treasures on Earth, where moth and rust destroy, and where thieves break in and steal. But store up for yourselves treasures in Heaven, where neither moth nor rust destroys, and where thieves do not break in or steal." Jesus is certainly not against rewards in Heaven. He is very much for them and warns believers against wasting our resources in this life when we will receive a much better return with our investments in Heaven.

Some Christians are uncomfortable with the idea that they will be judged in Heaven and some will be rewarded more than others. Christians who do not understand this teaching miss the heart of God and the intent of Heaven. In Heaven the sin nature from Earth which includes coveting and jealousy will no longer be present. Therefore, the citizens of Heaven rejoice with those who have been rewarded for their earthly service and sacrifice. Like any good father loves to reward his children for good behavior, so our Heavenly Father plans to reward His children for all they have done in His name.

Two books that influenced me greatly are Heaven by Randy Alcorn and Suffering, Martyrdom and Rewards in Heaven by Josef Ton. I highly recommend these books to anyone desiring further study on the subject of Heaven.

Josef Ton discusses the misguided belief that all Christians are treated and rewarded equally. "...suppose that there are two Christian women in a country in which Christianity is viciously persecuted. One of them keeps a low profile, so that few people, if any, know that she is a Christian. The other one is a shining light and many are converted through her testimony. As a result, she is persecuted, then arrested, tortured, and killed. My question is the following: When these two ladies arrive in Heaven will there be a difference in their eternal state?"¡

Josef Ton's question highlights what the heart and intent is of our Heavenly Father. If we, who are imperfect, understand the concept of rewards how much more our perfect Heavenly Father will reward those who have labored well for His namesake.

### Location Of Heaven

I grew up with an older brother and sister. One day we asked our mother where Heaven was. She wisely answered us, "Heaven is where God lives." This profound insight can be understood by both young and old. God is what makes Heaven perfect and good. Without God, Heaven cannot be Paradise! Before Heaven was God and God created the Heavens and the Earth. (Genesis 1:1, Revelation 10:6)

Revelation 21:2-3: tells us that one day God will make a new Heaven and a new Earth. God will live among men in this new creation and the New Jerusalem will descend upon the new Earth as the celestial city. In other words, Heaven will move from its present location down to the new Earth. Another way to understand this is that the move of Heaven will be expanded to include the new Earth and God's capital city of Jerusalem will be upon Earth. Therefore, the present location of those who have died and are in Heaven with God will change locations when the new Heaven and new Earth are established. God's presence in the new Earth will literally bring Heaven to Earth.

The Bible establishes that all this is to happen after the future judgment of the saints and those condemned to Hell. The Apostle Paul's letter in Romans 8:19-23 illustrates the picture that all of creation anticipates the completion of our redemption in eternal Paradise upon the new Earth.

The story in the gospels of the rich man and Lazarus describe the immediate destination of the poor man Lazarus with Abraham in a present Paradise. The rich man is separated by a great chasm and is in Hades. Some translations use the word Hell. This is a temporary abode since we are told at judgment Hades will be thrown into the bottomless Lake of Fire. We also know that the new Heaven and Earth are coming so that Abraham and Lazarus are in a temporary dwelling for the saints of God.

Therefore, when studying Heaven in the Bible it is helpful to differentiate between Biblical references to the present and the future Heaven (new Heaven and new Earth) still to come.

# Part Six: Chapter 24

### Fearless Love: Meditation

Ephesians 1:7-8, In Him we have redemption through His blood, the forgiveness of our trespasses, according to the riches of His grace which He lavished on us. God gave us the greatest gift the world has ever seen; salvation. We could live a million years and never earn or repay this gift. Our good works are first acts of gratitude in worship of the goodness of God. Second, our works are acts of wisdom knowing that a God who so lavished forgiveness upon us wants to reward us for obedience. Salvation is your sure destination because it is not based upon your good works. Thank the Lord today for His loving mercy that before His eyes God you are completely forgiven. Pray for Muslim friends who mistakenly think they must work for salvation when God wants to give them heaven so that they can begin to build heaven on earth in lives full of love and good deeds.

### Fearless Love: Endnotes

i    Josef Ton, *Suffering, Martyrdom, and Rewards in Heaven*, (Wheaton, IL: Romanian Missionary Society) pg 133

*Fearless Love Notes:*

*Fearless Love Notes:*

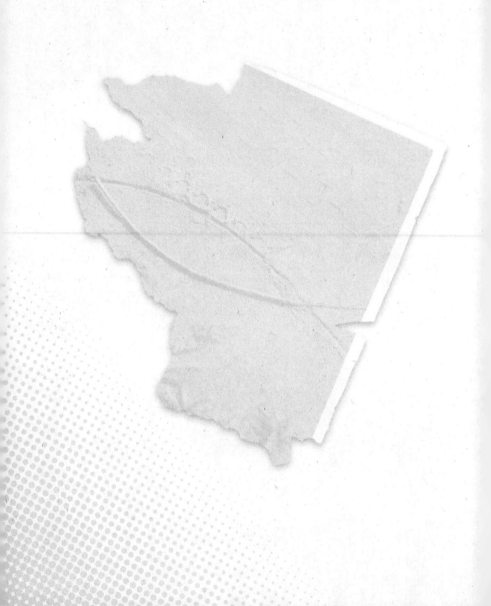

# CONDITION OF THE
## *Christian Martyrs In Heaven*

Revelation 6:9-11 is the most direct reference in Scripture regarding God and how he honors His martyrs. "When the Lamb broke the fifth seal, I saw underneath the altar the souls of those who had been slain because of the word of God, and because of the testimony which they had maintained; and they cried out with a loud voice, saying, 'How long, O Lord, holy and true, will You refrain from judging and avenging our blood on those who dwell on the Earth?' And there was given to each of them a white robe; and they were told that they should rest for a little while longer, until the number of their fellow servants and their brethren who were to be killed even as they had been, would be completed also."

Randy Alcorn in his book Heaven makes 21 astute observations regarding the martyrs in Heaven from Revelation 6:9-11. *i*

1. When these people died on Earth, they relocated to Heaven. (v. 9)
2. These people in Heaven were the same ones killed for Christ while on Earth. (v. 9) This demonstrates direct continuity between our identity on Earth and our identity in Heaven. The martyrs' personal history extends directly back to their lives on Earth.
3. People in Heaven will be remembered for their lives on Earth. These were known and identified as ones slain "because of... the testimony they had maintained." (v. 9)
4. "They called out" (v. 10) means they are able to express themselves audibly. This could suggest they exist in physical form, with vocal cords or other tangible means to express themselves.
5. People in the intermediate Heaven can raise their voices. (v. 10) This indicates that they are rational, communicative, and emotional-even passionate beings, like people on Earth.
6. They called out in "a loud voice," not "loud voices." Individuals speaking with one voice indicate that Heaven is a place of unity and shared perspective.
7. The martyrs are fully conscious, rational, and aware of each other, God, and the situation on Earth.
8. They ask God to intervene on Earth and to act on their behalf: "How long... until you judge the inhabitants of the Earth and

avenge our blood?"(v. 10)

9. Those in Heaven are free to ask God questions, which means they have an audience with God. It also means they need to learn. In Heaven people desire understanding and pursue it.

10. People in the Intermediate Heaven know what's happening on Earth. (v. 10) The martyrs know enough to realize that those who killed them have not yet been judged.

11. Heaven dwellers have a deep concern for justice and retribution. (v. 10) When we go to Heaven, we won't adopt a passive disinterest in what happens on the Earth. On the contrary, our concerns will be more passionate and our thirst for justice greater. Neither God nor we will be satisfied until his enemies are judged, our bodies raised, sin and Satan defeated, Earth restored, and Christ exalted over all.

12. The martyrs clearly remember their lives on Earth. They even remember that they were murdered.

13. The martyrs in Heaven pray for judgment on their persecutors who are still at work hurting others. They are acting in solidarity with and in effect interceding for, the suffering saints on Earth. This suggests that saints in Heaven are both seeing and praying for saints on Earth.

14. Those in Heaven see God's attributes ("sovereign...holy and true") in a way that makes his judgment of sin more understandable.

15. Those in Heaven are distinct individuals: "Then each of them was given a white robe" (v. 11). There isn't one merged identity that obliterates uniqueness, but a distinct "each of them."

16. The martyrs' wearing white robes suggest the possibility of actual physical forms, because disembodied spirits presumably don't wear robes. The robes may well have symbolic meaning, but it doesn't mean they couldn't also be physical. The martyrs appear to have physical forms that John could actually see.

17. God answers their question (v. 11), indicating communication and process in Heaven. It also demonstrates that we will now know everything in Heaven.

18. God promises to fulfill the martyrs' requests, but says they will have to "wait a little longer." (v. 11) Those in the intermediate Heaven live in anticipation of the future fulfillment of God's promises.

19. There is time in the intermediate Heaven. (vv. 10-11) They are aware of time passing and do not know the future but experience the present as it is happening.

20. The people in Heaven have a strong familial connection with those on Earth, who are called their "fellow servants and brothers." (v. 11)
21. Our sovereign God knows down to the last detail all that is happening and will happen on Earth (v. 11) including every drop of blood shed and every bit of suffering undergone by his children.

### The Rewards For The Martyrs Of Jesus Christ

The Bible does not give an exhaustive list of the specific rewards given to the martyrs but we are given hints of what these will be. Above we saw that Revelation 6:9-11 identifies two specific rewards. First the martyrs shall be "under the altar." The martyrs are given a resting place of honor and remembrance in Heaven, for the altar stands in front of the throne of God. Throughout the Old and New Testament the altars of God were a place of blood sacrifice. The altar in this reference is connected to the blood sacrifice of the saints for the testimony they maintained for Jesus Christ. God keeps the martyrs front and center before his throne and in the sight of all of Heaven as a constant reminder of their blood sacrifice. He will not let their sacrifice go unanswered nor without due reward and tribute. The reference to "under the altar" may be only symbolic and not a physical location but this does not diminish the value and honor God bestows upon the martyrs. Either way this is what the Apostle John "sees" in his vision and records it in Revelation.

We see this honor demonstrated by God in the first recorded martyrdom of Jesus' disciple named Stephen in Acts 7. While Stephen is facing death before a hostile crowd for his witness of Christ he declares, "Behold, I see the Heavens opened up and the Son of Man standing at the right hand of God." (Acts 7:56) This is the only record in Scripture of Jesus standing at the throne of God. This vision further shows the merited value of martyrdom before God. Stephen receives an immediate honoring reception at the throne of God. Jesus stands with focused attention and anticipation to receive His beloved Stephen.

It is also interesting to note the victorious scene in which this story is recorded. In spite of the obvious gore from the presumed blood and pain involved in Stephen' death, Luke, the author of Acts, focused on the ecstatic vision of Stephen who sees the Heavens opened to be received by Christ himself. Stephen's life could not be taken but given, for he utters the words, "Lord Jesus, receive my spirit!" The story ends with love and forgiveness in which Stephen in full cognitive control says, "Lord, do not hold this sin against them!"

## Part Six: Chapter 25

Back in Revelation 6 we are told that the martyrs are given a white robe. Robes symbolize righteousness, position, honor and identity. They are set apart with these robes so that all of Heaven may give them tribute.

Not only will the martyrs be given a robe but they will also be given a crown. (Revelation 2:10) Crowns represent glory and authority. So we are given clues that the martyrs will be given specific authority and power in Heaven.

Revelation 2:26 specifically says that those who overcome will be given authority over nations. In the new Earth (Heaven) there will be nations of people and the rulers of those people will be the martyrs from this present Earth.

The Scripture also promises a multifold return for the martyrs to compensate for the earthly loss of wife, children, and homes. And He said to them, "Truly I say to you, there is no one who has left house or wife or brothers or parents or children, for the sake of the kingdom of God, who will not receive many times as much at this time and in the age to come, eternal life" (Luke 18:29-30). We can have great assurance that the martyrs of this world will receive the equivalent of mansions in Heaven for the loss of their property here. We are told by Jesus that there is no marriage in Heaven (Mark 12:25) and yet Luke 18:30 promises the greater return for the loss of an earthly wife for the sake of Christ. Although we·are not told the details of this reward we can deduce that the familiar relationships (wife, children, parents) in Heaven will be even deeper, more fulfilling, more passionate and intimate than the relationships of this present Earth. Those who have lost family members because they refused to recant their faith will be given greater companionship than ever before. Those who have lost believing family members, temporarily by death, can look forward to their reunion in Heaven with anticipation of greater fellowship, enjoyment and companionship. Together with family members they will share in the discovery of the everlasting creation of God. What is magnificently clear in Scripture is that all the good we have experienced on Earth will be in Heaven in a greater and more perfect form.

Scripture also promises great joy to the martyrs. Sorrow and grief will be abolished by the ending of sin. Every tear will be wiped away and those who have sown in great loss will reap in great joy. Joy will radiate on the faces of the citizens of Heaven.

In summary, rewards for the martyrs on behalf of the Lord Jesus Christ are multifold. The martyrs will be given a place of honor before the throne of God. They will receive royal clothing for their attire and their heads will be crowned. They will have a special worship and intimacy with Christ. They will be given positions of authority to rule over nations and people. They will be given Heavenly estates of beauty.

The Scripture also promises a multifold return for the martyrs to compensate for the earthly loss of wife, children, and homes.

They will enjoy intimate relationships with family members and other citizens of Heaven. Their lives will be overflowing with joy and the blissful experience of life in Paradise with Jesus.

### Fearless Love: Meditation

If a black pen marked a spot on a white string that wrapped around the world, that pen mark could represent this life and the white string would represent eternal life. Like the flash of lighting in the sky is the length of this life in contrast to eternal life. The experiences of this life and the things important here become very dim in the light of eternity. Even the pain and suffering is distant with one look into heaven. In the midst of the pain and suffering of Stephen's stoning he saw heaven. His thoughts were immediately riveted not to himself but to those stoning him. Love overcame suffering and pain and gave an eternal perspective. The perpetrators were on a path that missed heaven and they needed forgiveness for their sins. (Acts 7:60) The very presence of God in Heaven gives perspective of His love and justice. Colossians 3:2, "Set your mind on the things above, not on the things that are on earth."

# Part Six: Chapter 25

## Part 6 Group Discussion And Contemplation

Pray: Pray to receive insight into the Father heart of God and His desire to reward His saints.

*Optional Audio Book: Play Disc 3 , Track 18 ,*
*The Rewards For The Martyrs—for seven minutes*

A vast majority of Islamic countries have extreme poverty. Illiteracy is high in most of these nations. The only assurance of salvation within Islam is martyrdom. With these factors in mind why do you think it is attractive for Muslims to die in jihad? If you were a Muslim and lived in one of these nations which of the rewards for paradise would be most attractive to you? Why?

Why do you think Muslim women are attracted to martyrdom? Why would parents raise their children to be martyrs? What reward do parents receive when their children die?

In your own words how would you summarize the difference between Islamic martyrdom and Biblical martyrdom? Discuss the similarities and differences between the motivation of martyrdom in Islam and Christianity.

Hebrews 11:6 (ESV): "And without faith it is impossible to please him, for whoever would draw near to God must believe that he exists and that he rewards those who seek him." Why do you think scriptures connect faith in God with God's rewards of those who seek Him? Why does God want to reward His children?

In your opinion what do think most Christians believe about "rewards" in heaven? Why do you think rewards from God are seldom taught?

Does the forgiveness of our sins have anything to do with our good works? Why or why not?

How will our obedience, sacrifice, love and faith shape our experience in Heaven? How do you feel about the idea of other saints in heaven being rewarded greater than you? Do you feel that rewards in heaven should all be the same or that some, like persecuted believers, should be rewarded for their greater sacrifice?

Why do you think God's presence in Heaven is key to the perfection and greatness of heaven? Could heaven be paradise without God? Why or why not?

Reread Revelation 6:9-11. Why do you think God revealed to us in scripture that the martyrs have an audience with Him? What does this imply about the current state of heaven? Is this situation something to be concerned about or rejoice in? Why or why not?

Out of the 21 observations from Randy Alcorn regarding Revelation 6:9-11 what particular one surprised you the most? Why?

How is justice on earth related by the martyrs and their relationship with God in Revelation 6:9-11? How does this picture of God and the martyrs show us God's mercy?

If people understood God's principle of rewarding their deeds of sacrifice and love how do you think it would change their priorities?

## Part Six: Chapter 25

Share your understanding of the Bible's teaching of rewards in heaven before this study. How has your insight into rewards in heaven for the martyrs changed?

If Muslims understood the teaching of the Bible regarding God's rewards for martyrs do you think this would affect the Islamic world? Do you think this is a teaching that needs to be shared with Muslims? Why or why not?

**Witness:** Talk to your spouse, family, friends, or church on how to begin to share this principle of rewards with others. Recommend this study book to a friend this week or give it away as a gift.

**Personal Application:** Begin to think of ways that you hope to be rewarded by God in heaven. Put into action God's principles of rewards and take steps of faith this week to serve, give, care, speak up and ultimately sacrifice for the good of others. Look for other scriptures in the Bible that talk about rewards in heaven and think about their implications for your life.

**Digging Deeper:** Check out Randy Alcorn's book's and resources on "Heaven" (Available on www.SpiritofMartyrdom.com)

**Ending Prayer:** Pray through the points and insights that you gained.

### Fearless Love: Endnotes

i   Randy Alcorn, *Heaven*, (*Wheaton, IL: Tyndale House Publishers, Inc*) *page 65-67 www. epm.org, www.randyalcorn.blogspot.com*

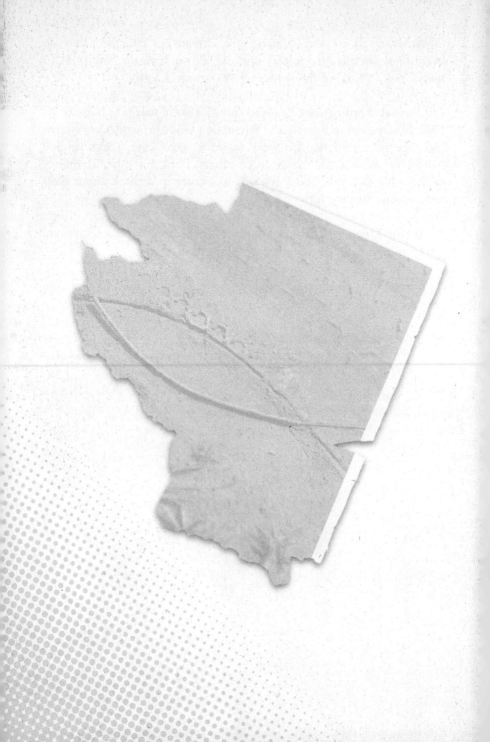

# Part Seven:
# FOR THE LOVE
## of Muslims

*Fearless Love Notes:*

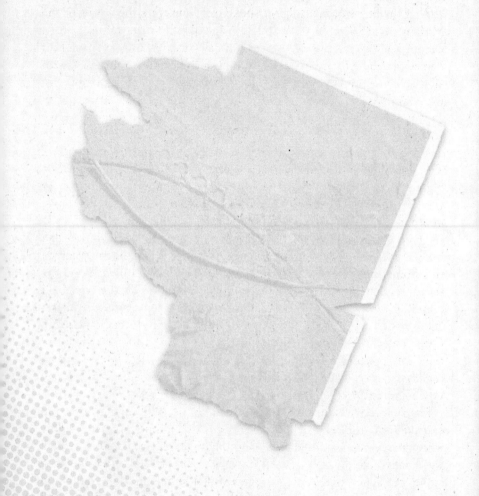

# EGYPTIAN MUSLIM
*Finds Peace*

### Witnessing Steps 1-3

Hamadi was born to an Egyptian Sheik. Like all good Muslims the first words his father spoke over him were the words of the Muslim creed as he dedicated his son to Allah. He was raised to be a devout Muslim. He prayed five times a day, fasted during the month of Ramadan and he tithed 2.5 percent of his money to the poor. Even with all this he did not have peace in his soul. Hamadi never felt that his sins were forgiven. He tried to become more pious. He studied the Qur'an and attended prayers at the mosque and would listen to the conservative teachers of Islam. Still, his thirst for peace would not be quenched. He decided to practice Sufism, a sect of Islam that practices meditation. Through meditation and spiritual incantation he sought to experience a higher spiritual reality of peace with Allah. At the age of twenty-five he was able to go on his first Hajj, the pilgrimage to Mecca, Saudi Arabia, in order to worship Allah at the Kaba stone.

The Kaba stone or called black stone is believed to be given by Allah from Heaven to Adam in the Garden of Eden. When Adam received this stone from Heaven it was pure and white. During Noah's flood the stone was lost, but then Allah led Abraham to rediscover the stone and reestablish it in today's Mecca, Saudi Arabia. It is a seven foot diameter cube-shaped stone in the heart of the Islam's holiest mosque on Earth. Over the years the stone has turned black as it has absorbed the sins of the pilgrims worshipping. The Hajj is certainly one of the great spiritual highlights of a Muslim's life. Every year over two million Muslims journey to worship in Mecca.

Hamadi looked forward to his Hajj as he had high hopes and expectations to draw near to Allah and have his sins forgiven. People were everywhere, clothed in their traditional religious garb. Hamadi was finally able to work himself forward to the blessed and holy Kaba stone. He kissed the stone, as required of Muslims in Hajj, and stood back. Nothing happened. He had expected a great flood of peace and confidence to wash away his sins. In his heart he could tell that there was still a hole of darkness. Great disappointment swept over him. Suddenly, he declared out loud, "Allah is not here, this is meaningless!" He turned and walked away from the great mosque of Mecca and from his faith in Islam.

# Part Seven: Chapter 26

I met Hamadi in Iraq the week Saddam Hussein was captured by American troops. He was in his late thirties, married and had a child. He had been arrested months before by Saddam Hussein's secret police for leading a Christian house Church. Because he was a Muslim convert to Christianity he was especially mistreated and beaten during his 30 days in prison. Hamadi related to me how he had come to Christ and why he lived in Iraq. After he left Mecca he lived a worldly life. He drank alcohol and womanized. He was working in Jordan when he met a Christian man at his place of employment. This man had something different about him. Hamadi began to ask questions. Various Scripture verses began to intrigue him like, Ephesians 2:8-9: "For by grace you have been saved through faith; and that not of yourselves, it is the gift of God; not as a result of works, so that no one may boast." Eventually, Hamadi understood the gospel and gave his life to Christ. This was the first day in his life that he was confident in his mind that his sins were forgiven and a great peace came over his heart

Because of Hamadi's new faith in Christ and living in an Islamic nation, he fled persecution from Jordan. His childhood home of Egypt was not safe for a convert, so he decided to move to Iraq. In Iraq he grew in his faith and eventually became a pastor and began a house Church for other Muslim converts. Today he continues to be faithful, even in the continued danger and unrest in Iraq.

In the past twenty years there has been more concerted prayer for the Islamic world than at any time in the history of Christianity. Many Christian organizations have major prayer focuses on the Islamic world and there are thousands of Christians now who fast during Ramadan on behalf of the Muslims.

When Muslims like Hamadi are beginning to have their eyes opened at the Kaba stone in Mecca, Christians can rejoice that God is hearing their prayers. Hamadi represents many others like himself who have reported similar spiritual revelations during their Hajj.

## Become Active In Loving Muslims To The Truth Of Jesus Christ

### 1. Pray And Fast.

The first step in reaching Muslims with the truth of the gospel is to pray and fast for them. Every year Muslims pray and fast during the daylight in Ramadan. Muslims are praying and fasting to an unknowable Allah. What a difference it can make when believers in Jesus are praying

and fasting to the known true
living Yahweh, the God of the Bible,
on behalf of Muslims. God is opening the eyes of Muslims
in more ways than ever before and He is inviting His children to be a
part of this great work. Mujahid and I challenge every believer in Jesus
reading this book to commit to pray every day for the Islamic world
that God's grace and truth will come upon Muslims. Consider fasting
during Ramadan. Fast during daylight while interceding to Jesus for the
Muslim world. Fast one meal a month or fast once a week in seeking
God's heart for the Muslim world. Any fasting and praying is better than
no praying.

### 2. Spiritual Warfare

Ephesians 6:12 (NIV): "For our struggle is not against flesh and blood,
but against the rulers, against the authorities, against the powers of this
dark world and against the spiritual forces of evil in the Heavenly realms."
Every believer in Jesus must understand the spiritual battle that rages for
the souls of Muslims. There is a demonic influence over Muslims' lives.
Jesus has given all authority to his children to come against these forces.
These demons are small compared to the glory of Christ, but we must
stand on our authority and with faith fight the good fight. The Qur'an
gives us insight into the demonic influence.

Surah 46:29: "And (remember) when We sent towards you (Muhammad)
a group (three to ten persons) of the jinn, (quietly) listening to the Qur'an.
When they stood in the presence thereof, they said: 'Listen in silence!'
And when it was finished, they returned to their people as warners." This
Qur'anic verse refers to jinn listening to Muhammad recite the Qur'an.
As they listened they were converted to Muslims and went to preach
the Islamic message in the spirit realm. (Surah 72 goes into more detail
about the conversion of the jinn) jinn are neither angels nor demons.
Muslims believe they are spirit beings and they can bring you blessings
or curses. The Bible makes it clear that spiritual beings are already aware
of the greatness of God and they are not to be "converted" as "warners"
or Muslims. These are demonic beings bringing influence in the spiritual
realm. Therefore, we find in the Qur'an that the jinn and the angels have
spiritual interactions and even companionship with Muslims and non-
believers. As believers in Jesus we know that these spiritual beings are
deafening the ears and blinding the eyes of their human hosts. We must
understand this spiritual interaction and pray with authority against the
evil spirits in the name of Jesus.

These spirits want to bring fear of the gospel and total submission to Allah. The Bible promises that we are given power over spirits by the blood and authority of Christ. The issue of the spiritual battle is authority. But authority is useless until it is exercised. A policeman does not have the strength, size or weight to stop the traffic at an intersection, but with one hand raised the traffic stops. Why? He represents authority. This authority is effective when Christians simply trust God's word and put His words into action. Jesus has given His authority to everyone of His living martyrs but like any authority we must exercise this power by faith in His word. As Muslims' spiritual eyes are opened we can begin to show them the freedom and love of God through Jesus Christ.

### 3. Build Bridges Of Friendship-Hospitality

The gospel is based upon relationships, first our relationship with God, next our relationship with others. Muslims have a culture of family identity. Community and hospitality are very important aspects of their lives. Christians must not merely talk about the gospel, but live it by taking the risk of developing friendships with Muslims. Consider the clever saying, "Your talk talks; your walk talks; but your walk talks a lot louder than your talk talks." When trust is built the Muslims' ears are open and there is a willingness to listen.

Friendships are not hard to build with Muslims, if you are willing to take the risk of getting outside your comfort zone. One of the languages of friendship in the Muslim world is a simple gift of service or a material gift. For instance, if your Muslim neighbor has not taken his trash out, and his trash bin is available on the side of his home a simple act of putting out the trash goes a long way. A pastor saw that his Muslim neighbor needed a new water hose and bought one for him. This began a dynamic relationship! Simple acts of kindness open hearts to love.

One of the highest values in the Muslim world is to share a meal together in the home. If you invite Muslims to your home and they accept the invitation, then they are accepting you as close friends and creating a bond that the Muslim community considers sacred. A brother in Christ, who works with Muslims in America, shared recently with me that he does not believe Americans will ever reach Muslims effectively. Why? Muslims respond to hospitality (meals in a home) and Americans do not practice hospitality with each other, much less with foreign Muslims. Do not underestimate the power of a meal in a home to produce fellowship, understanding, friendship and love. Take the risk! You will be blessed!

### Fearless Love: Meditation

John 1:46 "'Can anything good come out of Nazareth?' Philip said to him, 'Come and see.'" Some Christians might say what good can come out of Saudi Arabia. Today there are secret believers in Jesus living in Mecca, Saudi Arabia. Recently some Muslim Background Believers went on their hajj to Mecca and worshipped Jesus. You may feel that you are insignificant. You ask what good can come out of my town or city. God loves to confound the wisdom of the wise in this world. God loves the humble places and people. God enjoys surprising us and He gets more glory when it takes a miracle. God's love is redeeming people from places that only a few years ago no one could have imagined. Begin to pray with a big imagination today. If Jesus saw Nazareth as a good place to begin, He can start something big in your hometown and even more in your heart. Pray for God's love to touch the most unusual places and the hardest of fundamental Muslims.

*Fearless Love Notes:*

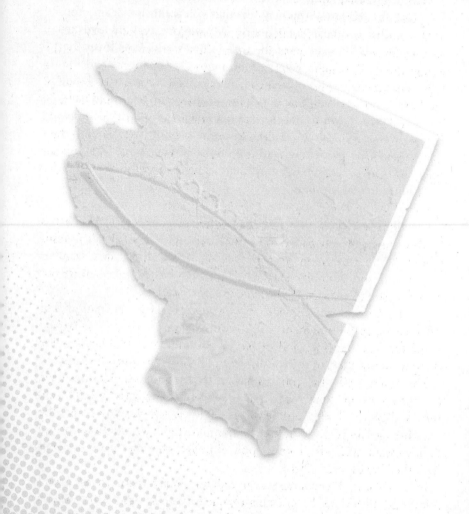

# GUIDANCE OF
*The Holy Spirit*

## Witnessing steps 4-7

*Guidance Of The Holy Spirit*

**4** Most Christians fear that they will not know what to say if they start a conversation with a Muslim or maybe they're afraid of saying the wrong thing. Remember God is the one in control and the Scripture tells us not to worry about what we will say when we speak on behalf of our Lord. God commands us to be faithful in trusting him and His Holy Spirit will lead us in our words and actions. Moses felt that he could not speak on behalf of God to the Egyptians. However, God gave him words that changed the demographics of Egypt forever. He will use your simply obedience also!

*5. Don't Debate: Testify!*

Changing a Muslim to a Christian is not our responsibility. That is God's concern. We are called to testify about our faith and hope in Jesus Christ. No one ever wins in this type of debate. If Muslims want to debate with me, I simply tell them I'm not interested in debating, but merely desire to share how I have been forgiven of my sins.

In our witness before Muslims, we want to avoid alienation. For instance, don't use statements like, "How can you be a Muslim? Do you know that the Qur'an is full of hatred and violence?" Statements like these will only alienate the Muslim from hearing the Truth of Christ.

The best attitude that you can have is that of a learner. Muslims have much to teach us. Remember that they were also created by Yahweh, the God of the Bible, and Jesus' grace is on the righteous and the unrighteous. Yes, their faith may be misguided, yet we will be surprised at how beautiful God's grace is upon all people when we open our eyes with the love of Jesus Christ.

In this spirit, I encourage everyone to simply learn to ask good questions of Muslims. Following are some easy questions: "What do you believe about Allah? What does the Qur'an say about going to Heaven? What makes a good Muslim and what makes a bad Muslim? You know that I am a Christian and trust the love and forgiveness of Jesus for my sins. I know that Muslims believe in Jesus as a prophet. What else does the Qur'an say about Jesus? Do you know what the Bible says about

# Part Seven: Chapter 27

Jesus? I pray for Muslims and hope to learn more, would you please tell me what is it like to be a Muslim in this country? As a Muslim, what do you think of Christians? What do you think Christians believe?" These are some questions to get us started, remember to listen intently without interrupting them. We will learn much if we listen with our hearts and our minds.

Once we allow a Muslim to express his or her opinion it is natural and culturally acceptable to share our testimony of why Jesus is so important in our lives. In this way we are coming beside the Muslim to learn and to teach. This becomes a non-threatening witness as we simply proclaim what Christ has done for us and thereby, plant seeds of love and hope in the Muslim's heart. We also grow in our understanding and compassion of our Muslim friend.

I have personally found it easier to speak with Muslims about God in the West than with secular Americans or Europeans. We must consider the second great commandment "to love our neighbor as ourselves." We would not be offended if a Muslim asked us about our faith. In the same way, many Muslims would be complimented if you sincerely asked them about their faith in Islam.

I met Alshad in Bangladesh. He had been baptized into Christ three years before I met him. Like most new believers he had little Biblical knowledge, but a big zeal to testify what Christ had done in his life. He did not care to debate Muslims but only wanted to share the gospel freely with those who would listen.

Alshad attended a fundamental Islamic school. Wahhabism is very conservative and is an orthodox sect of Islam. He studied the Qur'an and noticed that it talked about the prophet Jesus performing miracles of healing and raising the dead. The prophet Jesus is mentioned in the Qur'an over 120 times. The Qur'an never mentions that Muhammad performed any miracles. Muslims believe the only miracle performed by Muhammad is that of the Qur'an which he received from the angel Gabriel. Alshad thought Jesus was a greater prophet than even Muhammad and he wanted to know more about Jesus. He asked his teachers where he could find more teaching on Jesus. The Islamic teachers warned him that Christians worshipped Jesus and that they would lead him astray. He was commanded to be content to study only what the Qur'an teaches about Jesus. The warnings did not quench his curiosity. He secretly began to search for someone who could teach him about Jesus. This quiet search lasted a few months until one day he found a Hindu man who told him that he could teach him a little about Jesus since he owned a New Testament.

He secretly met with this Hindu man and together they read through the New Testament. After four years of meetings and reading through the New Testament the Hindu became a follower of Christ. Alshad's father became aware of his reading the Bible and he beat Alshad and told him never to meet with the man again. At the age of 22 Alshad moved to a big city in Bangladesh. He decided that he wanted to become a Christian. He found a Church, visited the priest, and asked how he could become a Christian. The priest understood the danger involved in converting a Muslim and told Alshad that since he was a Muslim he could not become a Christian. Alshad left the Church and feeling rejected by Christianity he never thought about Jesus again for 20 years.

Three years before I visited, a Muslim background believer in Jesus came to Alshad's village and preached the gospel. For the first time in his life he understood the message and desired to receive Jesus as Lord and Savior. He and his family were saved from their sins and when confronted by the village elders to come back to Islam, he refused. This earned him a beating with a cane that lasted for fifteen minutes. He and his family were forced out of the village and left homeless. He took the opportunity to go to a Bible school and learned about Jesus. Today he travels Bangladesh sharing the gospel of Jesus Christ with Muslims. At times he is beaten, spit upon, and threatened. At other times Muslims receive him with joy. He told me that in three years he has seen over 800 Muslims respond to the message of Jesus Christ.

He understands that his job is simply to testify to the Truth of Christ and what Jesus has done in his life. He shares that he does not need to debate with Muslims because the light of Christ will reveal the darkness of falsehood. He is called to be a faithful messenger.

One tool that I have found helpful is called How To Share Your Faith Without An Argument by Pastor Bill Faye. RBC ministries in Grand Rapids, Michigan has made his materials available. (www.rbc.org/Bible_study/discovery_series/booklet/31036.aspx)

### 6. *True Knowledge Of Islam*

The more we know about Islam and what Muslims believe, the more wisdom and knowledge we bring in sharing our faith with them. Seek out good books or listen to messages on Islam. Read a good translation of the Qur'an. We recommend The Noble Qur'an English Translation.

# Part Seven: Chapter 27

(Available at www.MuslimEducationCenter.com) Studying Islam for yourself will help you gain credibility with our Muslim friends.

### 7. Support Gospel Work In The Muslim World

Today there are many wonderful organizations that are working around the world with Muslims. We challenge every reader to consider supporting one of these organizations with your prayers, volunteer time and financial support. Mujahid and I are volunteer Associate Representatives with The Voice of the Martyrs. (www.persecution.com) David Witt oversees Spirit of Martyrdom ministries (www.SpiritofMartyrdom.com) Mujahid El Masih oversees Faith Covenant International. (www.ForTheLoveOfMuslims.com) We certainly recommend VOM , SOM or FCI as organizations worthy of your support. The main issue is to discern where the Lord is leading you to get involved. When you begin to invest your resources in places that are on the heart of God, you will be blessed.

**Fearless Love: Meditation**

Numbers 22:28 "And the LORD opened the mouth of the donkey..." God's love is so great for His people that He will use even peculiar mouths to proclaim His Truth. Alshad searched for months to find someone who would teach him about Jesus. Finally he found a Hindu man who owned a Bible. God can use a donkey, Hindu, Muslim, Buddhist, Jew, Atheist and even a Christian to proclaim His love for mankind. God created your month for His glory and praise. Your mouth works best when working as God designed. Open your month to share the love of Jesus Christ with the lost Muslim souls of the world. Maybe you can start with the lost and hurting associates at your work place or school. Pray that God opens your month today to speak His wonders and praise. Pray that God might use you in sharing His heart with others instead of using a donkey.

Fearless Love Notes:

*Fearless Love Notes:*

# MIRACLES

### Witnessing steps 8-11

8 *Miracles*
I heard the international speaker and writer Ravi Zacharias say that seventy percent of the Muslim background believers he has met experienced some kind of vision, divine dream or a miracle in their life as part of their conversion. Mujahid and I agree that in our experience this statistic is similar. We worship the living Lord Jesus, not a dead god. While the bones of Muhammad are still in the grave in Saudi Arabia, Jesus's tomb is empty. He rose from the dead. The Bible tells us that He is interceding for us at the right hand of the Father. Jesus still performs miracles today out of love for His creation.

### Healing Of Cancer – Mujahid

In 1996 I was involved in Christian meetings that were advertising, "Jesus heals and Jesus sets the captives free." Some Muslims heard about the meeting and wanted prayer, but they were afraid to go due to the danger of being caught by other Muslims at a Christian meeting.

A Christian sister who worked as a nurse in a Muslim hospital came to me and asked if I would come and pray for her patient. The nurse told me their story. This family had a ten year old son whose kidneys were failing. The Christian nurse said that if I came, we could meet safely at her home which was on the campus of the hospital.

I had mixed feelings. Joy that the Muslims wanted me to pray but fear that if the boy was not healed they would become angry and accuse the Christians of lying and make trouble for us. I sought the Lord for what to do. The Holy Spirit spoke to my heart and told me to go and preach the gospel. The Lord gave me a message for this family and their son. This Muslim family brought thirty relatives into the home of the nurse. I asked them. "Do you want a healing or a healer? If you only have a healing you might get sick again but if you have a healer you can ask him for healing anytime." They said they wanted a healer. Then I introduced them to Jesus as the healer! He is Lord and Savior. All thirty Muslims prayed to accept Jesus into their hearts. I prayed for their son and Jesus healed him!

Another time I was distributing Bibles in a city in Pakistan. I had a particularly difficult day with many rejecting the offer of free Bibles. I prayed that the Lord would guide me to some Muslims who would desire to take and read the Bible. Across the street was a shop to which the Holy Spirit directed me to go and offer a Bible. With high expectations I entered the shop and asked the owner if he would like to receive a free Bible. He said he was blind so he could not read the Bible. Momentary disappointment flowed into my mind. Suddenly the Lord gave me faith with a message. I asked him, "if you could see, would you read the Bible?" He replied, "of course if I could see I would read the Bible." I began to tell him how Jesus healed and brought sight to those who were blind and that Jesus could give him sight so that he could read. "Do you want me to pray for Jesus to heal your eyes and give you sight to read?" He said, "Yes, pray for me!" I prayed for him and Jesus restored his sight immediately! Great rejoicing came over this man! He asked me to also pray for his family. He not only received but paid for the Bible and promised that he would read it.

We do not "save" Muslims, God saves Muslims. In God's infinite love He is choosing to reveal himself in powerful ways to Muslim individuals. If God wants to show his power through miracles to Muslims then we simply need to be faithful servants and pray.

### 9. Use The Law

Muslims are taught that they are born as a blank slate and they either earn Heaven or Hell by their good or bad deeds. They do not understand that all people are born in sin and that God is holy and demands perfection. No one with sin will be in Heaven or approach the throne of God. Muslims need to understand that no matter how "good" they are they will never be holy and perfect and therefore never attain the standard of Heaven.

One of the questions I ask Muslims at every opportunity is, "What is the greatest commandment of God?" Most Muslims do not know and I share with them from the Bible how God said the greatest commandment is to love the Lord God with all your heart, mind, soul and strength. I ask them if they love God. Most say they do. Then I point out the Bible verse and logic that if you love God you will obey Him. "God has given us a standard of the Ten Commandments to help us know if we really love God or not." I say, "Let's test a few of them. The Bible says do not steal. Have you ever stolen? The size does not matter; have you stolen a pen from work; cheated on your taxes? Before God it is all unholy and it makes you a thief." Then I ask them if they have lied, hated, dishonored their parents, lusted. Most admit that they have failed on every commandment. I point out to them that if loving God is the greatest commandment then not loving Him is the greatest sin. "Therefore, do you admit that you have committed the greatest sin before a Holy God? If you were to die right now where must the Holy God of the universe send you?" One year in Turkey I was sharing with a young Muslim man. I came to this particular point and his physical body began to shake in the realization of the holiness of God and the judgment over him. He pleaded with us to pray for him in order that he might have his sins forgiven by Jesus.

God has written His law upon the heart of every person. As we share the laws of God it convicts their hearts of sin. People do not have to "believe" the commandments for them to be powerful. The law of God is powerful because it is the Truth. Let the Truth of the law do its work to bring conviction of sin.

Pastor Ray Comfort has influenced me regarding the Biblical principle of the law of God. He has some of the best and most effective gospel tracts available on the market. He also has tapes and books to effectively share the law and the gospel with others. One book I highly recommend by Ray Comfort is "Hells Best Kept Secret." He has teamed up with Actor Kirk Cameron to provide witnessing training and tools. You can find his web site at www.wayofthemaster.com.

### 10. *Spiritual Boldness*

1 John 4:18: "There is no fear in love; but perfect love casts out fear." The Lord spoke to my heart a couple of years ago that Christians in the West, especially America, have fallen into fear. I felt that the Lord spoke and told me to set the captives free preaching His message. The object of terrorism is to produce fear. The object of Jesus is to cast out fear. Love does not allow any room for fear.

The next verse, 1 John 4:19 says, "We love, because He first loved us." As Christ first brought his love to us we must bring love to Muslims. Muslims will not come to us. Fear paralyzes them. Love will drive the terror out of terrorists. Darkness is simply the void of light and fear is the void of love. Light drives out darkness and love drives out fear. Every Christian must pray for more love so that they might have more courage and boldness to seek out Muslims everywhere they go.

If we fear Muslims we will avoid them. For instance, if we fear the Muslim working at the local retail store we simply avoid shopping there and drive on to another retail outlet. By giving in to fear we disqualify

# Part Seven: Chapter 28

ourselves to be instruments of love and Truth to the Muslim world.

### 11. Speak, Pray, Act With Love!

The issue of love cannot be emphasized enough. St Paul said that if we do not have love then we are a resounding cymbal. Love needs to be the target in all our action when witnessing to Muslims.

If we love a Muslim then we can tell him or her anything. Even if what we say is inadvertently offensive to him or her. If a Muslim senses our love, he or she will simply think, "This Christian has no idea what he or she is saying but at least they love me." But if we do not have love for the Muslim, no matter how truthful our words are, he or she will not receive them. The Muslim may think, "This Christian just wants to convert me."

Therefore, love is the issue. The challenge that I ask every reader to consider is to pray that God will give you His love for Muslims. Consider praying everyday for five to fifteen minutes and purpose in your heart that you will not stop pleading to the Lord for a heart of love until God breaks your heart for Muslims around the world. I know that when God broke my heart for the Muslim world I began to weep for their pain. Once we have been broken we have earned the right to speak to a Muslim's life. Love costs everything! Your tears will be the ointment of healing for transformation of Muslims.

### Fearless Love: Meditation

Sabina Wurmbrand used to tell a story. Truth visited the world and wanted to share Himself with everyone, because Truth sets people free. He went knocking on every door. Most people were not prepared to meet Truth and were aghast at His sudden interruption. Some were offended and others angered. Truth was rejected, cursed, and abused. He became emaciated; his shirt was tattered. One day he came upon Grace. Grace was well feed and handsomely dressed. Truth asked, "Grace how is it that you have fared so well on this earth when I have suffered so much?" "Follow me." Grace replied. Grace knocked on the door and when the owner opened she saw Grace first. "Oh, please come in." Then she saw Truth. "Since you are with Grace you can come in also." Soon Truth was well fed and owned a new shirt. John 1:14(ESV) records, "And the Word became flesh and dwelt among us, and we have seen his glory, glory as of the only Son from the Father, full of grace and truth." As we bring love to a violent and hurting world let God's Grace lead God's Truth. When the lost hear you knock and open the door of their life, what do they "see?" Pray that God will fill you with the love of Jesus Christ. Pray for God's Grace and Truth to open the doors of Muslim homes.

*Fearless Love Notes:*

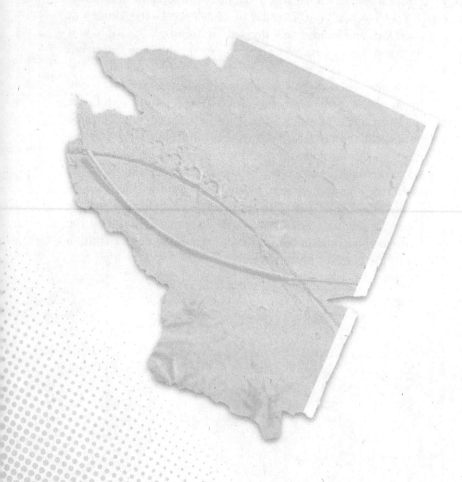

# USING
*Godly Wisdom*

## Witnessing Steps 12-17

### 12 *Godly Wisdom*

When we share with Muslims we want to speak to their soul. Truth is powerful and God gives us Truth to serve Muslims. Our goal should not be to prove to Muslims their ways are wrong but to show them that Jesus is right. As we trust God, He will give us wisdom in speaking to the problem of sin. For instance, to attack a Muslim with a complex argument regarding the authenticity of the Qur'an is not wise and is counterproductive. It is far better to show that Christ is the Word of God and He has confirmed His power by His death and resurrection.

### 13. *Culture*

To know a person's culture is to show respect for his values. Knowing culture can also become very practical. A British co-worker shared with me a humorous account of bringing his grown son to Iran. They had a dinner engagement at the home of Iranian friends. His son had been raised properly in British tradition to eat everything served on his plate. His father had forgotten to inform his son that in Iran it is appropriate to leave a little food on your plate when you are finished. Cleaning a plate of food indicates to the Iranian family that you are still hungry. His son is a big man standing at six foot four inches and can eat a lot. Sure enough as soon as the first plate was cleaned, the Iranian host quickly grabbed the plate and filled it. Again his son ate everything on the plate and again it was filled. His son was a guest in this country and did not want to be impolite so he forced himself to eat all the food on his plate. For the fourth time the plate was refilled. At this point, the father noticed the sweat on the forehead of his son and the very slow manner in which his son was eating. He whispered to his son that it was okay to leave food on the plate. His son was greatly relieved.

Some cultural issues in Muslim world are the same. For instance, a devout Muslim will not eat pork or drink alcohol. You will not want to serve those items if you invite them for dinner. Other cultural issues vary from country to country.

There are three simple ways to discover a Muslim's social mores. First, use the internet or library and read about the lives of Muslims. Second, contact an organization or ministry that works with Muslims and ask for resources and information. Last of all, ask Muslims themselves. Most Muslims love to share about their culture and would be more than happy to talk with you.

### 14. Language

Words can be a key to the heart of a person or may drive a person away. I like to call this learning the language of love. Knowing some Islamic words or concepts can further your understanding and build trust with your Muslim friend. For instance, "Salaam" in Arabic means peace and Muslims greet one another by saying "Salaam" or "Salaam Alakum." To greet another Muslim with this greeting can be a gesture of friendship and respect. The name of Jesus in Arabic is Isa. Knowing certain Arabic words can help to communicate ideas.

Knowing what not to say is just as important. To speak disrespectfully about Muhammad or the Qur'an when talking to a Muslim will be seen as offensive and not a very good way to build a relationship.

When witnessing the love of Christ to Muslims we must keep the final goal in mind at all times. The goal is to build relationships. God has called believers to the ministry of reconciliation. That is reconciliation of mankind to God and to each other. The gospel is communicated best by the depth of our relationships. When a Muslim knows that you love and care for him you have earned the right to share the gospel with him. Like most people, Muslims will share their pain, hurt, and insecurities when they know we can be trusted.

### 15. Sending Bibles To Muslims In Islamic Nations

Recently The Voice of the Martyrs launched a program to send New Testaments directly to Muslims within Islamic nations. Bibles, envelopes, stamps and addresses are all purchased on the web (www.Biblesunbound.com). Via international mail Muslims will receive a New Testament right to their home.

### 16. Share Written Testimonies Of Muslim Background Believers

There are many testimonies available today in books, audio or on the internet. We have set up a web site full of great testimonies on DVD, audio and print to give to Muslims. Go to www.MuslimEducationCenter.com to purchase them. I highly recommend these books to have available as a gift for Muslims. In the Den of Infidels are testimonies of eight Egyptian Sunnah Muslims. The last testimony in the book is a former terrorist who persecuted and murdered Christians. Desperate for God, is the sequel book of testimonies of Iranian Muslims who have come to Christ.

Samy Tanagho is a dear Egyptian friend. He has written the book; Glad News! God Loves You My Muslim Friend. His book deals with the theological objections that Muslims need answered in coming to faith in Christ. Again, you can find this book and many other resources at www.MuslimEducationCenter.com. This web site has been created to distribute testimonies to seeking Muslims.

I encourage you to order these books or similar materials. Consider keeping them easily accessible like in your car. Pray that God will lead you to Muslims. As your paths cross with Muslims, present one of these books as a gift. Let them know you're praying for them! Tell them about the web site. I do this on a regular basis and continue to be blessed by the positive reception of most Muslims.

### 17. *Share This Book With Others*

The Spirit of Martyrdom is written to be used as a tool. Many people today are interested in both Islam and martyrdom. This book will help Christians grow in their personal faith and deepen their understanding of Islam. Last of all, we encourage you to give this book to Muslims who are seeking peace with God.

(Partial proceeds of this book will go to projects to reach Muslims with the Gospel. Go to www.SpiritofMartyrdom.com)

I pray all these ideas will challenge you to reach out to Muslims. I can promise that as we reach out many blessings and surprises will come in ways that we would never have imagined. Mujahid and I desire to leave every believer in Jesus with this charge; "Go to the Muslim world and give'm Heaven!"

# Part Seven: Chapter 29

### Fearless Love: Meditation

Proverbs 11:30, "...And he who is wise wins souls." The wisest men and women of the world are champions of love. God wooed you to His love that you might win others to faith. In the Islamic world today millions of men and women are risking their lives for a Semite man from the Middle East. Both are willing to die. One man is the Semite Arab named Muhammed who advocated violent jihad and that Muslims fight unto death against their enemies on behalf of Allah and Islam. The other man is the Semite Jew named Jesus. The saying, "It is not what you know but who you know," is the difference of life and death when it comes to knowing Jesus. Winning a Muslim terrorist to know and follow Jesus is homeland security. Are you living wisely today? Is your life about winning souls to the Kingdom of Christ love? Pray that you can begin to use the stories and suggestions in this book to win Muslims to the good news of Jesus Christ.

**Part 7 Group Discussion And Contemplation**

Pray: Pray to receive boldness, inspiration and courage to witness the love of Jesus to Muslims.

*Optional Audio Book: Play Disc 3, Track 19,*
*For The Love Of Muslims—for five minutes*

Why was Hamadi so disappointed at the Kaba stone in Mecci, Saudi Arabia? What did he expect to experience and why? Millions of Muslims make the Hajj each year but not all are disillusioned like Hamadi. Discuss possible ideas of why Muslims have a variety of experiences. How does this testimony illustrate the grace of God?

Have you experienced a dramatic answer to prayer in your life? How did God answer your prayer? Have you fasted? If yes, share how you fasted and what you learned. Why do you think prayer and fasting is so important in ministry to the Muslim world?

The analogy of a policeman directing traffic was related to spiritual warfare. Discuss the similarities between these two areas and what can be learned from taking physical authority as related to taking spiritual authority.

What do you think is the Bible's idea of hospitality? Why is hospitality so difficult for most people? What are the major blocks for you to reach out in friendship, giving and hospitality to a Muslim? What would need to happen in your life to take steps of friendship and outreach to a Muslim?

In your witness of Christ are you afraid to speak out because you do not know what to say? Have you ever had a situation that words came to your mind and month that you knew was divine intervention? Share that experience. "Speaking up for Christ is more an issue of trust than knowledge." Do you agree with this statement? Why or why not?

Before you were a believer in Jesus Christ did you ever have someone debate you about the things of Christ? Was this helpful or not helpful? Why or why not? Why are questions and listening an effective way of communication?

Before this study, what other books have you read on Islam? Why are books and testimonies important in our witness of Jesus Christ? Are there other materials you can recommend for the group to read? Share what they are and how these other materials are helpful.

Have you supported a Christian ministry outreach before with prayers and finances? Share your experience and how you were blessed. Are there other organizations reaching out with love to Muslims? Share your knowledge and recommendations. When supporting an organization what characteristics are most important for you to consider?

Have you ever experienced a miracle from God? What happened? Is God obligated to work miracles? Why or why not? How do the miracles in Muslim lives today illustrate God's love for the Muslim world?

In your opinion do most people in the world feel they are overall "good" and deserve heaven? Explain your answer. How do you think most people reaction when they hear the ten commands quoted? Why? Why are the ten commandments so important in sharing Christ? When did you first feel convicted of your sin? What happened?

How has fear disqualified you from sharing the love of Christ with another person? How has fear kept you from engaging in the lives of Muslims?

How has this book study helped you develop a greater compassion and/or love for Muslims? Has this study helped you overcome some fear?

"Truth is powerful, but God gave us Truth so that we might love." What do you think this statement means? How do we use Truth as a tool of love to the Muslim world and avoid using Truth as an instrument of power and intimidation?

Have you ever had an embarrassing or humorous experience from a cultural misunderstanding? Share your story. Why is it a blessing to discover other people's culture?

What hot button words in English can be very offensive or communicate love and further relationships? What issues or words are emotionally loaded within the Christian cultures that are either positive or negative? How can you use your words to communicate respect and care for Muslims?

Have you ever given a Bible or book of testimonies away as a gift? Do you think that giving a Bible or testimony book away to a Muslim would be a good way for you to witness the love of Jesus Christ? Why or why not?

# Part Seven: Chapter 29

Can you think of someone who might be blessed by reading this book when you are finished? Discuss who you might give your book to and why you think they would be interested in reading it.

**Witness:** Decide on one idea from the seventeen listed that you can do this week. Plan on sharing your experience at your next meeting or with some friends. E-mail comments@SpiritofMartyrdom.com to tell us what happened.

**Personal Application:** Hesitation from a public witness of your faith is usually rooted in fear. Ask God to reveal any fear hiding in your heart and help you root out the fear with God's love.

**Digging Deeper:** Check out the "Bridges" curriculum produced by the Crescent Project and possible training and missions trips. Go to www.spiritofmartyrdom.com/purchase.php for the Bridges curriculum and click the link ministries for training and missions trips.

**Ending Prayer:** Pray through the points and insights that you gained.

*Fearless Love Notes:*

*Fearless Love Notes:*

# SPIRITUAL
## Foundations of Islam
### (With Contrast To Biblical Christianity)

We have provided this appendix as a tool, for those who need a basic understanding of the fundamentals of Islam with some contrast to Biblical Christianity.

Islam is an Arabic word meaning "submission to Allah" and it is described as a "deen" in Arabic, meaning "way of life" and/or "religion."*i* Allah is the Arabic name for the "Supreme Being." Allah is understood to be all powerful and sovereign over all things. Therefore, all things should be submitted to Allah. (i.e. "way of life") There is a way to get dressed. There is a way to cook and prepare your meal. There is a way to get married. There is a way to raise your children. Another way to understand Islam is that it is a system of life. Islam is a religious belief system, an educational system, an economic system, a cultural system, an artistic system, a jurisprudence system, and a political system.

I invite every Christian to think of the word *ISLAM* as an acrostic, remembering that *love* is what is going to transform Muslims:

**I**

**S** incerely

**L** ove

**A** ll

**M** uslims

Islam is a philosophical or theological system. Muslims are the believers in Islam. Muslim means slave of Allah or submitted to Islam. Muslims are the people within the Islamic system, and many Muslims only understand Islam as a culture or way of life as opposed to a theological system or choice. There are an estimated 1.2 billion Muslims in the world today.*ii*

### Muhammad

Muhammad lived from 570AD-632 AD. He is the founder and great prophet of Islam. Both his father and mother died when he was young. Muslims believe that he was a direct descendent of Abraham through the lineage of Ishmael. He lived in the region of

> **Most Muslims have never read their holy book called the Qur'an to understand it. (Even though they must recite and memorize the pronunciation of the words within this book.)**

# Appendix

Arabia as a merchant trader. He was influenced by Christian Nestorians and Monophysites. (Both groups are considered heretical by Christian Orthodoxy because they did not hold to the divinity of Jesus Christ.) He was also influenced by Jews, Zoroastrians, and idol worshippers of the Arabian region. By tradition Muhammad at the age of 40 was visited by the angel Gabriel in the year 610 AD. Muhammad was told to recite or memorize the words spoken by the Angel Gabriel which were the direct words of Allah. These visitations happened over 22 years in which Muhammad received various portions of the Qur'an.

## Qur'an

The Qur'an is believed to be the exact Arabic words of Allah. Allah communicates in Arabic and it is the language spoken in Paradise. The Qur'an's focus is the duty of Muslims in worshipping Allah. The Qur'an dictates the requirements of life for every Muslim. The Qur'an clearly communicates that Allah cannot be known and in fact it is discouraged to "know" Allah in Islam. For instance, Allah is never described as a Father in the Qur'an. The Qur'an does have general descriptions of Allah—even being all merciful. However these are vague descriptions since Allah is beyond human understanding and can do whatever He wills. There are 114 chapters in the Qur'an; the chapters are called Surahs. The Qur'an is the greatest authority in Islam.

Most Muslims have never read their holy book called the Qur'an to understand it. (Even though they must recite and memorize the pronunciation of the words within this book.) There are several reasons for this. First, it is estimated that nearly 35% of the population in predominate Islamic nations are illiterate. Some Islamic nations have an illiteracy rate of over 60%.iii Second, the Qur'an is believed to have all authority and to be spoken only in Arabic. The Arabic of the Qur'an is formal Arabic and not the common tongue spoken today. Only one-fifth of the Islamic world is native Arab. Therefore, four-fifths of the Islamic world must learn a language that is not their native tongue and is very difficult. Third, the Qur'an does not encourage critical thought and study of itself. Surah 5:101-102: "O you who believe! Ask not about things...a community asked such questions, then on that account they became disbelievers."

## Hadith

The Hadiths are the teachings and traditions of Muhammad. These stories were recorded by the followers of Muhammad. They are stories of how Muhammad lived out his faith as the prophet of Islam and what he taught in regard to faith and life for a Muslim. There are volumes of Hadiths. The Hadiths are the second greatest authority in Islam.

## Salvation

There is no sure way (only one exception explained later) for a Muslim to know he has a place in Paradise when he dies. Consider the following two Hadiths. From the Hadith of Abu Hurayrah Mishkat Al-Masabih: "Allah's Messenger (peace be upon him) said, "There were two men among the Banu Isra'il who loved each other, one of whom engaged ardently in worship while the other called himself a sinner. To the sinner He said, 'Enter Paradise by My mercy,' and to the other (worshiper) He said, 'Can you forbid My mercy to My servant?' He replied, 'No, my Lord.' Then he (Allah's Messenger) said, 'Take him (worshiper) away to Hell.'"

From Sahih Bukhari, Volume 4, Book 55, Number 549: "So a man may do deeds characteristic of the people of the (Hell) Fire, so much so that there is only the distance of a cubit between him and it (Hell) ...and enters Paradise. Similarly, a person may do deeds characteristic of the people of Paradise, so much so that there is only the distance of a cubit between him and it (Paradise) ...and enters the (Hell) Fire."

Allah is unknown to mankind and all powerful and will judge as He desires. It is recorded that Allah has predestined some for Hell and some for Paradise. Therefore, since you cannot know the mind of Allah it is impossible to know whether you have salvation or not. The Qur'an does not have a clear plan of eternal security for mankind. 1.2 billion Muslims go to bed every night without peace that their bad deeds are forgiven. Muslims' eternal destination is completely in the hand of Allah alone. His ultimate will is impossible to know and therefore Islam is fatalistic in its belief regarding Heaven or Hell. Many Muslims live with a deep dread and fear of death since they do not have assurance of salvation.

In contrast, the Bible declares assurance of salvation to all Muslims, who place their trust in the gospel of Jesus Christ: John 20:31 "...but these have been written so that you may believe that Jesus is the Christ, the Son of God; and that believing you may have life in His name." Certainly when Muslims' eyes are opened to understand that forgiveness of sins and salvation is guaranteed by a revealed loving God, this is truly good news!

# Appendix

## Sin

Islam teaches that every person is born as a clean slate. It does not teach that every human is born with original sin as Christianity does. Islam teaches that there are two angels that watch every person. One angel records the good deeds and the other angel records the bad deeds. On judgment day the books will be weighed. If their good deeds outweigh their bad deeds then the hope is that their good deeds will help sway Allah in giving eternal life in Paradise to Muslims. Muslims must work their way to Heaven.

Surah 2:286: "Allah burdens not a person beyond his scope. He gets reward for that (good) which he has earned, and he is punished for that (evil) which he has earned." This is a typical verse communicating the spirit of the Qur'an which teaches that Muslims will either earn Paradise or earn Hell.

## Five Pillars

The Five pillars of the Islamic faith are acts of good works. Each pillar is seen as adding points to your good works score. For instance, every time a Muslim says the creed, he or she works off twenty bad deeds as recorded in the Hadith.

1. Creed: The Islamic creed is the supreme deed. It is seen as coming to belief in true monotheism. It is very easy to become a Muslim. If a person were to go to a mosque and repeat the creed, "There is no other God but Allah, and Muhammad is His prophet" before two Muslim witnesses that person would be given a Muslim name and considered a convert. By contrast, it is not so easy to leave Islam.

2. Prayer: A Muslim is required to pray five times a day. These prayers are scripted. There is a way they wash themselves before prayers. They must bow towards Mecca; they must kneel correctly and say their prayers in Arabic. Many of the prayers are quoting from the Qur'an. If any of the traditions of prayer are not done properly their prayers are cancelled and Allah will not hear them. The prayers start as early as four or five o'clock in the morning before sunrise and end after sunset as late as ten o'clock. The prayers demand absolute submission.

3. Fasting: Every Muslim must participate in a yearly thirty day fast called Ramadan. Muslims may not eat food, drink liquid or have sexual intimacy during the daylight hours. Every Muslim must participate with only a few exceptions for Muslims with health issues.

4. Alms: Muslims are required to give two point five percent of income or more to the poor, widows or orphans. The propagation of Islam is also included in Alms giving. Therefore, giving to organizations like Hezbollah, Hamas, or Al-Qaeda are acts of righteousness. This pillar helps explain the rationale of why millions and billions of dollars are going to terrorist organizations.

5. Pilgrimage: Muslims must make a pilgrimage called Hajj to Mecca and Medina in today's Saudi Arabia, the traditional place that Muhammad received the Qur'an from the angel Gabriel. They worship at the holy sites and see this pillar as one of the spiritual highlights of a Muslim's life.

While entrance into Paradise is not clear, entrance into Hell is. The Qur'an makes it clear that if Muslims do not perform the five pillars then they are paving for themselves a path into Hell.

### Martyrdom for Islam

Surah 3:157-158: "And if you are killed or die in the way of Allah, forgiveness and mercy from Allah are far better than all that they amass (of worldly wealths). And whether you die or are killed, verily, unto Allah you shall be gathered." Martyrdom is the trump card for every Muslim. The night before September 11, 2001 the Muslim terrorists in Florida were womanizing and drinking alcohol, both forbidden in Islam. They were doing this on the night before they knew they would die and face judgment before Allah. They were devout Muslims, how could they justify such unrighteous behavior? They were going to die as martyrs in jihad and therefore all their sins were covered by the deed of martyrdom.

Martyrs do not have to face judgment. The books of the two angels are destroyed and they go straight to Paradise. They are given the pleasure of seventy-two virgins. They get to intercede before Allah for seventy family members to join them in Paradise. These are just a few benefits for Islamic martyrs. (All this is discussed more in depth in *Part One on Jihad*.)

### MERITS OF ISLAM IN CONTRAST WITH THE GOSPEL
*Are Islam and Christianity Equally Yoked?*
Islam denies the tenants of the Orthodox Christian faith.
Jesus was not God.

1. Surah 3:59: "Verily, the likeness of Isa (Jesus) before Allah is the likeness of Adam. He created him from dust, then (He) said to him:

# Appendix

'Be!'-and he was."

2. Jesus was not crucified; therefore, He did not rise from the dead. Surah 4:157: "And because of their saying (in boast), 'We killed Messiah Isa (Jesus), son of Maryam (Mary), the Messenger of Allah,'-but they killed him not, nor crucified him, but the resemblance of Isa (Jesus) was put over another man (and they killed that man)... For surely; they killed him not...'"

3. There is no forgiveness for sin in Jesus; he was just a messenger of Allah. Surah 4:171: "O People of the Scripture (Christians)! Do not exceed the limits in your religion, nor say of Allah aught but the truth. The Messiah Isa (Jesus), son of Maryam (Mary), was (no more than) a Messenger of Allah and His Word... Say not: 'Three' (trinity)! Cease!" This verse directly denies the divinity of Jesus and calls him merely a "Messenger of Allah" (or a Prophet). The logic follows that if Jesus is not divine, he cannot speak for God and cannot declare our sins forgiven.

## Is there equality of people in Islam?

Surah 3:110: "You (true believers in Islamic Monotheism...) are the best of peoples ever raised up for mankind...." Most Muslims would see Judaism as the elementary school, Christianity as the high school and Islam as the university. The teachings from the Qur'an are not as gracious as many Muslims may express. The Qur'an equates non-Muslims as worse than animals. Surah 8:55: "Verily, the worst of moving (living) creatures before Allah are those who disbelieve..."

This doctrine of Islamic superiority creates a modern problem for fundamental Muslims. Allah is considered the sovereign being, yet he has allowed blessings to the Christian and Jewish world in the past 400 to 500 years (medically, educationally, economically and militarily). The only explanation for this dilemma, according to fundamental Islamic teachers, is that many cultural Muslims are in disobedient against Allah. These modern Muslims have not been fulfilling precise requirements of life and duty according to the Qur'an.

## Muslims should NOT befriend a Christian or a Jew.

Surah 5:57: "O you who believe! Take not as Auliya (protectors and helpers) those who take your religion as a mockery and fun from among those who received the Scripture (Jews and Christians)."

*Does Islam preach peace?*

Islam instructs Muslims to fight until all their opponents submit. Surah 9:29: "Fight against those who believe not in Allah, nor in the Last Day, nor forbid that which has been forbidden by Allah and His Messenger (Muhammad) and those who acknowledge not the religion of truth (Islam) among the people of the Scripture (Jews and Christians), until they pay the Jizyah with willing submission, and feel themselves subdued." Surah 5:33: "The recompense of those who wage war against Allah and His Messenger and do mischief in the land is only that they shall be killed or crucified or their hands and feet be cut off..." Surah 2:193: "And Fight them until there is no more Fitnah (disbelief and worshipping of others along with Allah)..." Surah 47:4: "So, when you meet (in fight-Jihad in Allah's Cause) those who disbelieve, smite (their) necks till when you have killed and wounded many of them, then bind a bound firmly (on them, i.e. take them as captives)." This particular verse justifies the beheading of infidels--Christians, Jews and non-Muslims.

In contrast the Bible commands believers to have a spirit of humility and to bring the Truth forth in love. The judgment of God against sin is already over the head of all Muslims who have not had their sins forgiven through the blood of Jesus Christ.

Jesus commands us to be fruit inspectors. Matthew 7:15-20: "Watch out for false prophets... By their fruit you will recognize them... Likewise every good tree bears good fruit, but a bad tree bears bad fruit." Muhammad claimed to be a prophet of God and to have the revelation of God. Therefore, Muhammad's revelation must be put to the test.

## Fruit Test

*Name one Islamic ruled country today that is not a major abuser of human rights?*

Saudi Arabia—is considered the holiest place on Earth for Islam. There is not an official Christian Church throughout the whole country of Saudi Arabia. Even the American military and embassy personnel cannot have an official Christian service in Saudi Arabia. Free religious expression is nonexistent in Saudi Arabia. Open Door's "World Watch List," stated that in 2008, Saudi Arabia was the number two worst nation of persecution in the world. (http://sb.od.org)

Iran—is a country that lacks in minority rights and freedom of expression.

Egypt—is considered the intellectual center of Islam, yet higher education has not brought freedom, but oppression upon Christians and other minorities. Christians have been murdered or falsely jailed

# Appendix

and Churches have been destroyed. Children have been kidnapped and forced to become Muslims and parents have had little legal protection in reclaiming their children.

Sudan—The leaders have wanted to make their country a pure Islamic nation for the past 20 years. There is an estimated 2 million dead from the ensuing war against the mostly Christian southern Sudan.

What about the fruit individuals have tasted under Islamic rule? In 2000, Darcie Gill, a VOM representative, was in Sudan when they rescued Kamarino. Kamarino was a ten year old boy who had gone out to find food with three other boys that day. They came across Islamic Sudanese soldiers who chased them into the elephant grass. The boys hid and the soldiers lit the grass on fire. Kamarino's three friends fled the fire and they were gunned down. Kamarino decided to trust God and stayed in the fiery bush. The fire swept over the place where he was hiding and over fifty percent of his body was burned. The soldiers left him for dead. The villagers later found him and tried to help, but the closest medical facility was five hours away by truck and there was no transportation. They prayed to God for help. About this time Darcie and the VOM team were led to visit this village. They heard the story and were able to transport Kamarino to the hospital. At the hospital he was given medical attention. He was given food, clothing and an education. I have a beautiful photograph of Kamarino taken a year later dressed with a big smile on his face. His wounds have healed; he is not hungry and he is learning to read.

What are the fruits that Kamarino has experienced with Islam? Terror, nightmares, murder, suffering, scars, hunger, illiteracy. What if Kamarino would have been a Muslim boy? What would the ministry team have done? They still would have brought him to the hospital because the Bible calls Christians to love their enemies, but there is no such command in the Qur'an. Let the fruit speak for itself.

## Does Islam bring freedom?
*Freedom is a universal human desire. What does the Qur'an teach on specific issues of freedom?*

## Women
Surah 2:282 is the foundational verse that declares that the witness in court of one man equals the witness of two women. It is taught in the Hadith that a woman has the intelligence of half of a man. Women are handled

as property and may be physically punished. Surah 4:34: "As to those women on whose part you see ill-conduct, admonish them (first), (next) refuse to share their beds, (and last) beat (scourge) them (lightly, if it is useful)..."

### Freedom of Speech or Press

There is no freedom of press to criticize Islam. Surah 9:12: "But if they violate their oaths after their covenant, and attack your religion with disapproval and criticism then fight (you) the leaders of disbelief."

### Racial Equality

Surah 3:106-107: "On the Day (i.e. the Day of Resurrection) when some faces will become white and some faces will become black; as for those whose faces will become black (to them will be said): 'Did you reject Faith after accepting it? Then taste the torment (in Hell) for rejecting Faith.' And for those whose faces will become white, they will be in Allah's Mercy (Paradise), therein they shall dwell forever." Why is Allah concerned about the color of one's skin as part of his judgment?

### Freedom to change religions

Surah 4:89: "They wish that you reject Faith, as they have rejected (Faith), and thus that you all become equal (like one another). So take not Auliya (protectors or friends) from them, till they emigrate in the way of Allah (to Muhammad). But if they turn back (from Islam), take hold of them and kill them wherever you find them." Any Muslim who leaves Islam is to be put to death.

### Freedom to question Islam

Surah 5:102: "Before you, a community asked such questions, then on that account they became disbelievers." Muslims are not to question the teachings of Islam.

### Freedom from Sin

There is no tolerance of actions that are considered disobedience. For example, in Islam countries alcohol is illegal, mixed swimming is illegal, modest dress is mandatory, books, music, videos and movies are censored. If you are caught stealing, the Islamic law calls for the cutting off of your hand so that the person guilty can literally not steal with that hand anymore.

# Appendix
## What is Jihad

This issue is discussed in much greater detail in Chapter 1. Here is a quick summary. Literally, jihad means striving or struggling in the propagation of Islam from the individual to the world. The Noble Qur'an's footnote of Surah 2: 190: "Al-Jihad (holy fighting) in Allah's Cause (with full force of numbers and weaponry) is given the utmost importance in Islam and is one of its pillars (on which it stands). By jihad, Islam is established, Allah's Word is made superior, and His religion (Islam) is propagated. By abandoning jihad (may Allah protect us from that) Islam is destroyed and the Muslims fall into an inferior position; their honor is lost, their lands are stolen, their rule and authority vanished. Jihad is an obligatory duty in Islam on every Muslim, and he who tries to escape from this duty, or does not in his innermost heart wish to fulfill this duty, dies with one of the qualities of a hypocrite." Every Muslim on Earth is in jihad according to the Qur'an and Islamic teaching.

There are four major types of jihad. Against ones base-self, against Satan, against infidels, against the hypocrites (Those who pretend to practice, but do not follow the teachings of Islam).

Every human being is divided into one of two groups. You are either a Muslim or non-Muslim. There are two groups, called two houses, within Islamic Theology:

1. The House of Islam - Muslims
2. The House of War – which groups all non-Muslims: Muslims are at war against non-Muslims

## Judgment Day

Sahih Al-Bukhari, Hadith No. 2926 Allah's Messenger said, "The Hour will not be established until you fight against the Jews, and the stone behind which a Jew will be hiding will say, 'O Muslim! There is a Jew hiding behind me, so kill him." Islam teaches that the glory of Islam will come to the world in one day when all Muslims will stand up and fight against non-Muslims. Those who do not confess Islam that day will be slaughtered. Allah will help in this victory by giving rocks and trees mouths to cry out to the Muslims on the hunt to find the Christians and Jews who have escaped. The end of the story for Islam is a blood bath which brings the dominion of Islam over the world.

## The Return of Jesus

Surah 4:159: "...And on the Day of Resurrection, he [Isa (Jesus)] will be a witness against them." Sahih Al-Bukhari Hadith No 3448: "Isa (Jesus),

Son of Maryam (Mary) will shortly descend amongst you (Muslims), and will judge mankind justly by the law of the Qur'an (as a just ruler); he will break the Cross and kill pigs and there will be no Jizyah." Islam teaches that Jesus will return and lead Muslims in judgment against the Christians breaking their crosses for the audacity of making Him equal to God.

### Does Muhammad bring Peace and Love?

Muhammad conquered Mecca with the sword. He slew all those who would not submit to Islam. In contrast, Jesus gave his life in Jerusalem for his enemies.

### What about Qur'anic verses regarding peace and tolerance?

Muhammad in the first ten years of his ministry as a prophet only had 200 followers and wisely taught respect and honor for other people's faith. For instance, Surah 2:256: "There is no Compulsion in religion..." This verse was later abrogated (canceled). After ten years he began to teach jihad and continued to practice jihad until his death (632 AD). During the time of jihad Islam began to spread throughout Arabia. Therefore, fundamental Muslim theologians must deal with direct contradiction in the Qur'an. When the Qur'an contradicts itself, how do Muslims handle it?

## Abrogation

The Rule of "Abrogation" simply defines the latest revelation as having the greatest authority. For instance, Surah 2:109: "Many of the people of the Scripture (Jews and Christians) wish that if they could turn you away as disbelievers... But forgive and overlook till Allah brings His Command." This sounds like a Judeo-Christian principle that could be found in the Bible. However, this verse is abrogated or superseded as footnoted in The Noble Qur'an by Surah 9:29: "Fight against those who believe not in Allah, nor in the Last Day, nor forbid that which has been forbidden by Allah and His Messenger, and those who acknowledge not the religion of truth (i.e. Islam) among the people of the Scripture (Jews and Christians), until they pay tribute tax with willing submission, and feel themselves subdued."

## The Christian Crusades

The teachings of Jesus condemned the spirit of the Crusades. ("Blessed are the peacemakers..." or "turn the other cheek...") Jesus commands

# Appendix

Christians to love their enemies and bless those who curse them. The Christian Crusades were wrong.

But the Qur'an condones violence and forced conversion. Fight/ Jihad!

*Allah of the Qur'an vs. Yahweh of the Bible, are they the same God?*

Surah 9:14: "Fight against them so that Allah will punish them by your hands and disgrace them." John 3:16 in the Bible states "For God so loved the world that He gave His only begotten Son." Surah 3:54: "And they (disbelievers) plotted [to kill Isa (Jesus)] and Allah planned too. And Allah is the best of those who plot." (This Arabic word for plot is pronounced Makareen and can be translated as deceiver.) Allah of the Qur'an deceives. Yahweh (God) cannot lie. Titus 1:2: "...the hope of eternal life, which God, who cannot lie, promised long ages ago."

Many characteristics in the Qur'an of Allah are in direct contradiction of Yahweh in the Bible. These stark differences show that Allah of the Qur'an is not the same Supreme Being as Yahweh of the Bible.

## Appendix Group Discussion And Contemplation
Pray: Ask God to give spiritual insight into the religion of Islam

*Optional Audio Book: Play Disc 4, Track 18,*
*Interview with David Witt and Dr Mujahid El Masih—for 11 minutes*

Islam is an Arabic word meaning "submission to Allah" and it is the way of life. In the general sense of this word, how is Islam similar or different from Christianity?

Islam teaches that the Qur'an can only be understood in the original Arabic language. The Bible can be translated into any human language to be understood and still considered the "Holy Bible." Why are there two different perspectives upon the holy books? What does this tell us about Islam's view of the Qur'an? What does this tell us of Christianity's view of the Bible?

Discuss the plan of salvation within Islam. How is it different from the plan of salvation as given in the Bible?

Islam boasts that Muhammad was just a man and is not to be worshipped. The creed of Islam is repeated daily, "There is no other God but Allah, and Muhammad is His prophet" Muhammad is revered in Islam. Do you think Muslims treatment of Muhammad is different from Christian's treatment of Christ? Why or why not? What constitutes worship of a person?

Can Islam and Christianity have spiritual unity? Why or why not?

# Appendix

Can Islam ever rule politically using fundamental Shariah Islamic law and avoid discrimination and human rights abuses? Why or why not?

Have you met Muslims who are very compassionate and peace loving people? Share what you know about them and the fruit of their lives. Would you consider peace loving Muslims fundamental or cultural Muslims? Why or why not?

Why do you think there is so little freedom in fundamental Islam? With fundamental Islam gaining in popularity around the world how do you think it will affect these cultures and countries? How will it affect Christians and the gospel witness?

Do you think Jesus of the Qur'an(Isa) is the same Jesus of the Bible? Why or why not?

Do you think Allah of the Qur'an is the same God as Yahweh of the Bible? Why or why not?

The Christian Crusades is one event of many horrible events in history that have been done in the name of Christ but contrary to the scriptures of loving our enemies. In what ways can the Body of Christ begin to bring healing and forgiveness for these past violations?

How has this study helped your understanding of Islam, martyrdom and God's love? Discuss the ways that this book study has helped increase your witness for Jesus Christ.

**Witness:** Keep informed. Sign up for the free The Voice of the Martyrs educational newsletter on the persecuted Church. Go to www.spiritofmartyrdom.com/contact.php to sign up.

**Personal Application:** Ask a brother or sister in Christ to partner with you in encouragement and prayer to continue to grow in courage regarding your witness of Jesus Christ. Seek ways that you can be stretched in your faith.

**Digging Deeper:** For more resources regarding Islam visit www.MuslimEducationCenter.com

**Ending Prayer:** Pray through the points and insights that you gained.

### Fearless Love: Endnotes

i     http://www.wordiq.com/definition/Islam

ii    http://islam.about.com/library/weekly/aa120298.htm

iii   http://www.uis.unesco.org/en/stats/statistics/UIS_Literacy_Regional2002.xls

# COME

## *Let Us Reason Together*

To keep informed, invest in the ministry of Spirit of Martyrdom, Faith Covenant International and The Voice of the Martyrs, or invite David Witt or Dr Mujahid El Masih as a speaker, please contact us at:

*www.SpiritofMartyrdom.com*
Spirit of Martyrdom
PO Box 101
Clarkdale, AZ 86324
Contact@SpiritofMartyrdom.com

## *Serving the Church; The Living Martyrs Witnessing Jesus Christ To Muslims*

Vision statement: Spirit of Martyrdom ministry:
Existing for the glory of God by serving the Church;
Assisting persecuted brothers and sisters globally, the living martyrs;
Speaking on behalf of our persecuted family;
Equipping Christians to serve as witnesses around the world;
Presenting Muslims with the witness of Jesus Christ.

Visit MuslimEducationCenter.com to view testimonies and materials to distribute to seeking Muslims.

# End notes
## Faith Covenant International Ministry

is a non-profit organization, which is dedicated to help the persecuted churches in Asia, Africa and the Middle East. Faith Covenant international is presently supporting close to one hundred churches, a Bible college, and Jesus Heals Medical Clinic in Asia. The main goal is establish the Kingdom of the Lord Jesus Christ.

Our Vision for the West and the Muslim World
1. To strengthen the churches in the West that they will take a firm stand for Jesus Christ.
2. Educate the church about the danger of Islam and how we can win Muslims for Jesus Christ.

To invite Dr Mujuahid El Masih or contact Faith Covenant International directly:

## www.ForTheLoveOfMuslims.org

Faith Covenant International
P. O. Box 2570
Parker, CO 80134
pastorelmasih@ForTheLoveOfMuslims.org

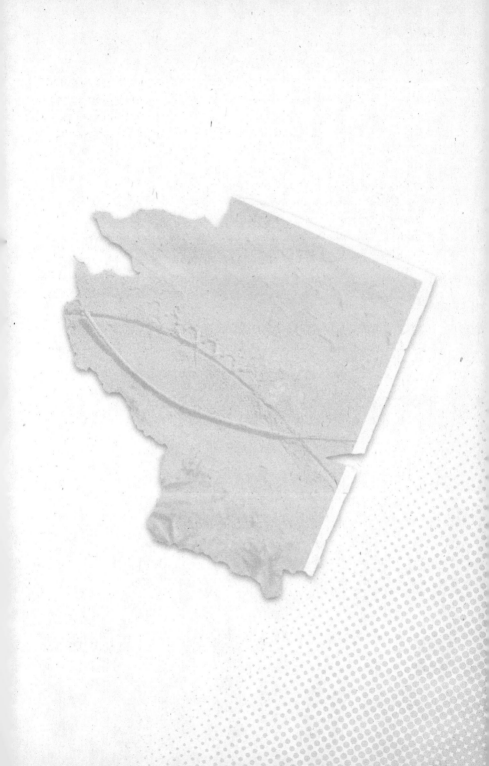

# About the Cover Photo

The photograph on the cover is a fish symbol used by Christians. Its history, in Christianity, dates back to the early persecuted Church—roughly 70-100 AD.

While in Columbia, the *Spirit of Martyrdom* team was walking to the gravesite where Wycliffe Bible Translator Chet Bitterman, a martyr, was buried. David and I were talking about the book, Fearless Love, when our guide (Alex—also a believer who had been persecuted) drove his motorbike on ahead of us inadvertently flipping a twig that had been embedded in the dirt. The inverted twig made the shape of the fish symbol.

The motorbike indentations in the dirt, the "accidental" flipped twig, the presence of our guide—a living martyr—made for me the perfect metaphor of the persecuted church. It was a symbol of the modern and primitive rolled up into the hand of Someone bigger—who makes stories out of the ordinary.

God, like our guide, leads His people down the dirty roads of life. He upends circumstances like the twig, (which for us can be chaotic) and creates out of chaos a symbol of His enduring love. We in return take note of those who have gone on before us and are strengthened by their stories and our love increases. Love catapults fear out of our lives.

The Christian fish symbol is a reminder that through God's presence, the lives of the saints, and our own experiences we learn to have *Fearless Love*.

By graphic artist Jay Myers